EXMOOR
RANGERS' FAVOURITE WALKS

EXMOOR
RANGERS' FAVOURITE WALKS

TWENTY-FIVE CIRCULAR ROUTES COMPILED
BY STAFF AND VOLUNTEERS OF
EXMOOR NATIONAL PARK AUTHORITY

EXMOOR BOOKS

First published by Frederick Warne 1979 as *Walks for Motorists*.
Revised and updated edition 1990 by Exmoor Books
Revised and updated edition 1992
Fourth revised and updated edition 1994
Fifth revised and updated edition 1996
Sixth revised, updated and retitled edition 1999
Reprinted 2001
This revised and updated edition published 2005 by Exmoor Books
Revised and updated 2011
Reprinted 2017

British Library Cataloguing-in-Publication Data
A CIP record for this title is available from the British Library

ISBN 978 0 86183 448 8

EXMOOR BOOKS
Exmoor Books is a Partnership Between
Halsgrove & The Exmoor National Park Authority

Halsgrove House,
Ryelands Business Park,
Bagley Road, Wellington, Somerset TA21 9PZ
Tel: 01823 653777   Fax: 01823 216796
email: sales@halsgrove.com

Part of the Halsgrove group of companies
Information on all Halsgrove titles is available at: www.halsgrove.com

Printed and bound in India by Parksons Graphics

Contents

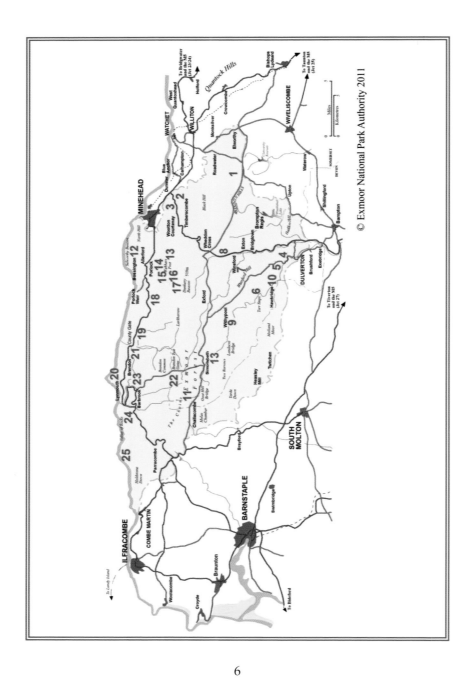

© Exmoor National Park Authority 2011

Introduction

For the casual walker Exmoor is one of the most attractive of Britain's National Parks. There are 625 miles (1005 kms) of public footpaths and bridleways and public access is permitted on thousands of acres of moorland and woodland. It lacks the mountainous heights of some National Parks but this is compensated for by the spectacle of the coast and its gorges and the friendliness and intimacy of the countryside and the relative mildness of climate, which makes Exmoor suitable for walking throughout the year.

The designation of Exmoor as a National Park does not mean total freedom for the walker, as most of its 267square miles (692 sq km) are still privately owned and where there is public ownership there is not necessarily open access. However, the National Park Authority has had considerable success in improving access and facilities for walkers and there is probably no comparable part of the country with such a well maintained network of trails.

The Exmoor National Park Authority was the first to introduce waymarking in Britain and you will find the national colour coding system for waymarks, which are coloured according to status of the route. The colours are yellow for a public footpath, blue for a public bridleway and purple for a restricted byway. These are known as Public Rights of Way, which you have a legal right to traverse. There are various other routes which have been negotiated with landowners through formal or informal agreements. You do not have the same legal rights on these paths but you may use them unless otherwise indicated. They are usually signed and waymarked but do not always appear on maps.

Outdoor recreation and access to the countryside were among the reasons for the establishment of National Parks. Today walking is seen as one of the ways in which to enjoy the 'special qualities' of these areas. Such qualities include fresh air, peacefulness, wildness and generally 'getting away from it all'. Exmoor is lucky in being relatively remote from large centres of population and, except in the few well known locations, does not suffer greatly from problems of excess numbers of visitors. However, traffic can be a problem and even a few vehicles can spoil the qualities which make Exmoor walks enjoyable. All of the walks in this book are circular, starting and finishing at a legitimate and recognised car parking area. They can, therefore, all be reached by car. Many, however, can be reached by bus, particularly between June and September, and it is well worth considering using a bus as a less stressful alternative to a car, a better way of enjoying the scenery and a way of reducing the pollution and noise that can lessen everyone's enjoyment. Public transport timetables are widely available in the area, including at National Park Centres. Another useful scheme is the 'Moor Rover', which will pick up within the West Somerset area of Exmoor National Park and drop off users at pre-arranged drop-off points anywhere on Exmoor; details are online or in the National Park Centres.

This book gives you a wide choice, covering most of the National Park, and there is plenty of opportunity for solitude. However, routes through some of the well known areas such as Dunkery, Tarr Steps, Dunster and Doone Country are well used and have become eroded in places. The National Park Authority maintains Public Rights of Way on Exmoor but resources are limited. The team of professional path workers needs your help to tackle wear and tear above normal maintenance requirements. There are a number of donation boxes in car parks, National Park Centres and places of accommodation. Please contribute towards the upkeep of paths used in this guide by making a donation.

The paths followed by this guide are generally maintained to a high standard. Where you do come across muddy patches, however, please try to keep to the main route. Going around muddy patches only contributes to erosion, making such patches wider and wider. For this reason it is advisable to wear walking boots on these walks. They also help to make your walks more enjoyable by providing support and keeping your feet dry. Wellington boots are an alternative for shorter walks, but a good lining of socks is recommended.

A recommended map is the Ordnance Survey Explorer (OL9) Map of Exmoor. The sketch maps and route descriptions in this book should be adequate for navigation but the detail provided by the Ordnance Survey map is a useful back up and tells you much more about what you can see from the walks. To assist in finding the start point of each walk, a six figure map reference is given. To find the place indicated on the map, take the first three numbers of the reference and relate them to the numbers along the top of the relevant Ordnance Survey map. For instance, if the first three numbers are 892, the reference line is two-tenths of a square east of the line marked 89 and runs downwards. Now take the second three numbers and relate them to the numbers running down the side of the map. If these are 416, the reference line is six-tenths north of a line marked 41 and runs horizontally across the map. The place indicated by the six figures is found where the two lines cross. In this case SS892416 is the reference for Dunkery Beacon - try it yourself. The SS refers to the map sheet, as the numbers are repeated on different sheets.

For many walkers, satisfaction is incomplete without the companionship of their dog. This is feasible on all these walks but, for the dog's sake and your own peace of mind, the dog should not only be under control but seen to be under control. Although your dog may have a long proven record of good behaviour amongst other animals, the animals do not know this and there have been horrific instances of injury to sheep, which have taken fright when dogs have merely shown curiosity, and much disturbance of ground nesting birds. On open country to which there is access under the Countryside and Rights of Way Act there is a right of access on foot but no automatic right of access for dogs. On all such open country dogs must be on a short lead.

A feature of Exmoor is the widespread use of horses. In a period of wet weather this can make parts of bridleways muddy. Most of the paths that are liable to heavy use by horses have been omitted from this book but you may encounter horses, and also mountain bikes, which can approach fast and silently. Horses and bicycles have a legal right to use bridleways and they may have permitted use of footpaths. Generally, there is no problem as long as the different users observe each other's rights and show courtesy.

Observance of the **Countryside Code** helps to avoid most problems:

Be safe – plan ahead and follow any signs

Even when going out locally, it's best to get the latest information about where and when you can go; for example, your rights to go onto some areas of open land may be restricted while work is carried out, for safety reasons or during breeding seasons. Follow advice and local signs, and be prepared for the unexpected.

Leave gates and property as you find them

Please respect the working life of the countryside, as our actions can affect people's livelihoods, our heritage, and the safety and welfare of animals and ourselves.

Protect plants and animals, and take your litter home

We have responsibility to protect our countryside now and for future generations, so make sure you don't harm animals, birds, plants or trees.

Keep dogs under close control

The countryside is a great place to exercise dogs, but it's every owner's duty to make sure their dog is not a danger or nuisance to farm animals, wildlife or other people.

Consider other people

Showing consideration and respect for other people makes the countryside a pleasant environment for everyone – at home, at work and at leisure.

National Park Rangers deal with the many issues that arise on public paths. Their task is not law enforcement but to ensure the job of the National Park Authority is achieved. This is:

- to conserve and enhance the natural beauty, wildlife and cultural heritage of Exmoor
- to promote opportunities for the understanding and enjoyment of the special qualities of Exmoor

Kennisham, Colly and Lype Hills
4 miles (6.5 kms)

Start: Entrance to Kennisham Hill Wood at Goosemoor on the Wheddon Cross road, OS map ref: SS964358

This walk in the Brendon Hills takes you through forestry plantations and across fields. In the latter part of the walk on Colly and Lype Hills, please take care to follow the route and walk around and not across fields. Lype Hill, at the western extremity of this walk, is the highest point in the Brendon Hills at nearly 1400 feet.

There are no very steep gradients on this walk but there might be a damp stretch in the lower part of the woodland. It is most important to keep dogs under control because in addition to sheep, large numbers of pheasants are bred in this area.

The starting point is 3 miles from Wheddon Cross at a junction with a road from Brompton Regis. Wheddon Cross is reached on the A396 from Dunster or Tiverton, or on the B3224 from Exford. Cars can be parked in the picnic site inside the woods on the right.

Start off along the forestry track, running directly away from the road. In front will be seen Croydon Hill with the largest Forestry Commission woods in the area. Keep straight on at the crossroads following the bridleway sign towards Luxborough. Halfway down the track looking left, there is a glimpse of the Bristol Channel with the mountains of Wales beyond. Carry on downhill to the edge of the wood and go through the gate immediately in front. Walk by the side of the hedge on the right until the hedge turns right.

As the hedge turns right, turn left to a gate with a signpost. Go

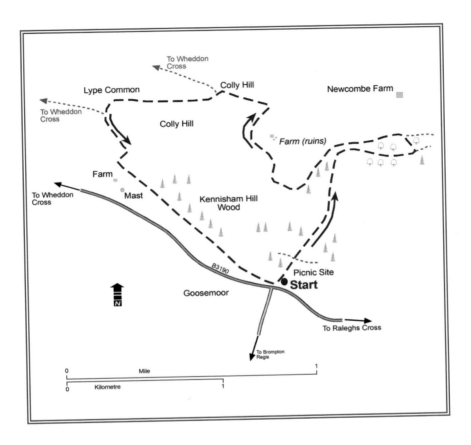

through this gate following the bridleway sign for Colly Hill. After a short stretch the track joins a forestry road. Turn right along the road following the signs for the bridleway. As the road meanders on through woodland used for rearing pheasants, listen out for the shrieking cries of the buzzards as they float over the landscape. After a short while the track opens up to a meeting of roads. Turn left following the bridleway signs for Colly Hill.

Opposite Newcombe Farm this runs into another wide forestry road. Turn left onto this road again following the bridleways signs for Colly Hill and from here onwards follow blue waymarks, climbing gradually through beech woodland with a brook down to the right. Near the top of the rise is a signpost showing the bridleway passing through a gate and into a meadow. Go straight through the gate and walk along the boundary of the meadow and wood. At the far end go through another gate and alongside the stream for a few paces before, crossing the stream and following the marked path up through a tangle of trees.

The blue waymarked path follows a sunken track steeply upwards to a gate out of the wood. Go through the gate and follow the fence on the right to the top of the field, which has a solitary tree and a ruined building on the left. This is a good time to take a breather. Looking back across the valley, the course of the path through Kennisham Wood can be traced, and looking ahead there are the Quantock Hills and the Mendip Hills beyond in the far distance. Now bear right through the gate and follow the bridleway sign towards Churchtown.

Follow the blue waymarked path along the left hand side of the hedge, pass through a gate and on past some ruined farm buildings. Still following the blue waymarks, take the left hand gate following the dilapidated hedge and wire fence curving round to the left. Ignore the first gate to your right and follow the fence line right round and uphill towards a long beech hedge line with a gate through it.

Go through the gate and on your right should be sign post. Follow the bridleway sign to Wheddon Cross via Pitleigh and head up across the field keeping close to the field boundary on your right. To the left is the very conspicuous landmark of the telecommunications mast at the western end of Kennisham Wood. This mast is a useful landmark because it can be seen from very many points in the eastern half of Exmoor.

After a short while a fence line cuts left across the field parallel to the path. Follow the fence line left until you reach a gate with a signpost nearby. Follow the bridleway signs to Wheddon Cross. The path follows the left hand field boundary and is waymarked. Go through the gate with the blue waymark and the quill logo (a marker for the Coleridge Way). The path continues straight ahead towards a gate with a signpost high up on the gate post. This is the renowned view point at Lype Hill with fine views of Dunkery Beacon and the Avill valley leading down to Dunster. It is also usually very windy and, if there is a nip in the air, your progress onto the last stage of the way will be accelerated.

After taking advantage of the magnificent views go through the gate and turn left to follow the fence line down hill. At the end of the field turn right to follow the fence line along to a gate giving access to a small field with farm buildings on the right. Go through the gate following the fence line close to the buildings and then go straight on through a gate onto forestry land. After the gate follow the bridleway sign to Kennisham Hill which leads along a wide forestry road running back to the picnic spot.

Dunster Park
3¼ miles (5 kms)

Start: Car park at Dunster Steep, OS map ref: SS993438

Dunster is one of the busiest villages in modern day Exmoor and it can be a relief to set off on one of the many footpaths radiating from its centre. The Yarn Market, standing in the High Street and proclaiming the importance of Dunster as a trading centre for wool, was built in the late16th century. It was damaged in 1646 during the 6 month siege of the castle in the Civil War.

Near at hand, the Luttrell Arms Hotel dates from the 16th century and commemorates the long association that the Luttrell family has had with Dunster. They purchased Dunster Castle from the Norman family of de Mohun in 1376 and retained it until 1976, when Col. Luttrell presented it to the National Trust together with 30 acres of parkland. The original castle was built in 1070 but none of this stands today. Most of the present building was completed in the 16th and 17th centuries, although the inner gatehouse is thought to date back to the 13th century. The Deer Park, over which this walk takes place, was enclosed by Henry Fownes Luttrell between 1755 and 1758 and many of the fine trees still standing in the park were planted by the same man.

To reach the start, turn off the A39 to enter Dunster on the A396 and the car park (pay and display) is at Dunster Steep, 100 yards from the junction on the left. Exit the car park by the steps adjacent to the toilets and follow the main road into the village, pausing to visit the Exmoor National Park Centre on the left. Follow the A396 through the high street, passing the Yarn Market. On reaching the

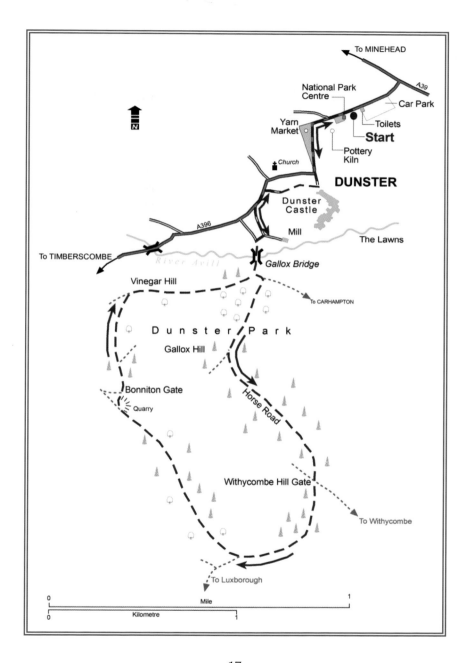

traffic lights, go straight on to climb the rise towards the castle. Turn right at the foot of the castle, and go straight on to rejoin the main road at West Street. Turn left, and follow the street down to the end of the cobbled pavement and turn left down Mill Lane.

After about 100 yards, turn right along the footpath between the new houses to Park Street. Turn left, passing picturesque Rose Cottage. Cross Gallox Bridge over the River Avill. The bridge is so named because it is the route to the crossroads beyond, where the public gallows are thought to have stood. Pass the thatched cottages on the right. At the Crown Estate Information Board bear left to Park Gate and pass through a kissing gate. Turn right, following the sign indicating a bridleway to Withycombe. At the next gate go straight ahead, keeping to the main path along the side of the stream. The stream vanishes and after some bracken covered slopes there is a conifer plantation on the right, mainly comprising spruce and larch with the native silver birch holding its own here and there. At the fork, follow the main path around to the left. The next landmark is a massive V shaped oak on the left. Keep to the main track.

Climb steadily and a stone faced bank on the left will indicate the end of this climb. Opposite the sign to Withycombe on the right, turn left to go through Withycombe Hill Gate and then turn immediately right to leave the blue waymarked path and follow a vehicle track, which runs parallel with the boundary bank on the right. As the path descends, the prominent feature in front is Black Hill. Still going downhill, this track sweeps round to the right with woodland on both sides and a drop on the left to a stream. There are some very fine specimen trees, both conifers and hardwoods, along this sheltered valley and a profusion of wild flowers along the banks of the stream, which is reached when the track joins another woodland road.

Keep straight on from this junction, following the restricted byway towards Bonniton. There is a gentle stroll now, keeping the babbling stream on the left. On the right there are some small quarries from which the stone for forest roads has been extracted. In the second of these quarries fork off to the right, opposite pasture. Now climb uphill on a forest road that has a variety of conifers on both sides. After a steady pull uphill, the road turns sharp right and then descends to another junction. Keep straight on, passing Bonniton Gate on the right and aiming for some splendid pine trees in front. From the middle of these pine trees, Grabbist Hill appears in front on the other side of the valley and it is surprising to note how much height has been gained since forking off at the quarry.

As the path starts to descend, fork left. Just after this fork it is well worth making a diversion to the small promontory in a clearing on the left. The view from here, especially in the direction of Dunkery Beacon (which is beyond Grabbist Hill) is a just reward for the effort. It is a steady descent from Vinegar Hill, with dense banks of rhododendrons below to the left. All along this section of path there are remarkable examples of a wide variety of trees, many of them planted 200 years ago. Amongst some cedars the path is joined by a blue waymarked path and shortly after this junction the outskirts of Dunster can be glimpsed down to the left. Very soon the path returns to Gallox Bridge after covering one of the most varied woodland walks that Exmoor can offer.

Dunster around Grabbist Hill
4½ miles (7 kms)

Start: Near Frackford Bridge, Dunster,
OS map ref: SS985433

On the previous walk, Dunster Deer Park, which lies to the south of Dunster, was explored; on this walk Grabbist Hill, which overlooks Dunster from the west, is climbed - as gently as possible! The walk also goes through majestic mature woodland above Alcombe.

The starting point for this walk is just off the A396 road from Dunster, 350 yards beyond the Forester's Arms and just before Frackford Bridge over the River Avill. On the right hand side of the road travelling towards Timberscombe there is a wide turning which is not signposted. Immediately after turning into this road, there is a small parking space on the left.

To start the walk, take the blue waymarked bridleway running up into the wood on the opposite side of the road. This path runs parallel with the Dunster road, climbing steadily past a recently cleared area on the right and oak trees on the left. Keep heading uphill until you reach a signpost. Follow the bridleway sign to Minehead & Wootton Courtney. Now there is an easy climb through Grabbist Coppice with a steep gradient down to the left into the Avill valley. Avill was the Saxon word for apple and this low-lying valley once sheltered several orchards.

From the first seat along this path, there are views of Dunster Deer Park to the left, with bare Black Hill beyond, and in front can be seen the extensive Forestry Commission plantations on Croydon

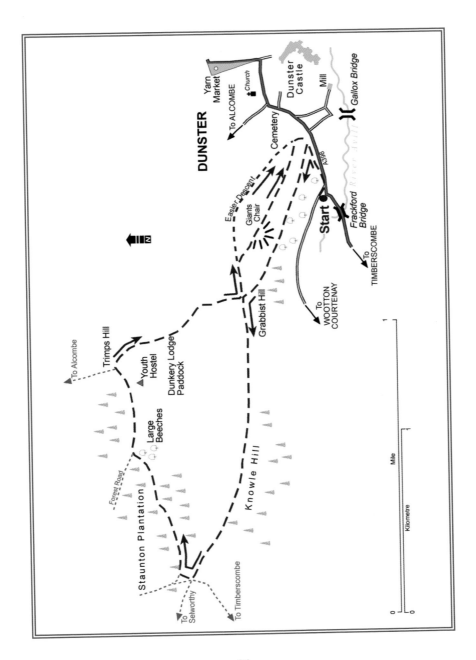

Hill. Not long after this seat there is a small plantation of beech and larch on the left where a signpost points the way upwards. Soon there is open hillside on the right and then there is suddenly a panoramic view of most of Minehead with North Hill on the left, the harbour under the hill, Butlins in front and the golf course running alongside the sea to the right.

Turn left immediately after the seat onto the wide track, going slightly uphill and still following the blue waymarks. It is open walking here and there are fine views to all points of the compass, especially east towards the Quantock Hills and north to Wales. Keeping on the wide track, the next landmark is a memorial seat and a helpful signpost. Follow the bridleway signed for Wootton Common. Now looking half right, nearly at the left hand end of North Hill can be seen the high point of Selworthy Beacon.

Just before the path climbs again to Hopcott Common there is a prominent junction with a signpost and vehicle barriers. Turn right towards Minehead, but don't follow the main track down the hill. Just as the track leaves the clearing there is a narrow path to the right which veers further away from the track and back across the bottom of the common. A bridleway sign at the bottom of the track points towards Alcombe; follow this track into the woods.

The going is easy now, on a wide track with occasional glimpses of the sea in front. As the path descends more steeply, larger pines are passed and then there are plantations of young spruce and larch. Numerous tracks and paths come in from right and left but the route to follow still carries on downhill, indicated by blue waymarks. Near the bottom of this descent, the path turns left by a large beech tree that has been scarred by the attention of previous passers by.

The path follows a stream for a while, then crosses it and comes to a forestry road. Turn right onto this road and follow alongside the stream until a memorial seat is reached on the left. Cross the stream here and continue on down the road in the same direction, passing the entrance to Minehead Youth Hostel on the right, following the bridleway signpost to Alcombe

About 400 yards below the hostel drive, turn sharply right to follow the path signposted to Alcombe Common. On the left is gorse-covered Trimps Hill, which is a blaze of yellow for a considerable part of the year. For a time it is a steady stony climb up and the path bends round to the right passing between two paddocks. Continue upwards for a short stretch until you reach the signpost. Turn left along the bridleway to Dunster

Continue uphill and along the path until it forks. Head straight on, avoiding the downhill path. On reaching a hunting gate with a blue waymark, do not pass through, but bear right on the wide track so that you follow a wire fence line. Near the crest of the hill is a signpost. Take the left hand fork keeping close to the fence line. 30 yards later a familiar spot will be encountered - the seat from which the first view of Minehead was obtained after climbing through Grabbist Coppice.

Bear left, keeping the National Trust 'Grabbist Hill' sign to your right and continue on for a short while until reaching a signpost. If it is wished to avoid an exceptionally steep and stony descent, best left to experienced walkers, fork left at this point and follow the blue waymarks on a steady descent through woodland to rejoin the original route by the cemetery. Even if not tackling the steep descent, it is worthwhile wandering along the ridge to enjoy in the breathtaking views.

If continuing down the steep slope then keep following the ridge, passing on the right a natural terrace known as the Giant's Chair.

The views from this ridge are even more spectacular with no trees in the foreground to break them up. Away to the right is Dunkery, to the left is the Conygar Tower which was built as a folly by Henry Fownes Luttrell in the 18th century and away in front is Bridgwater Bay with the conspicuous hulk of Hinkley Point nuclear power station.

Keep straight on and descend rapidly over grass and loose stone. This descent is very steep and should be made with care. At the bottom, with the cemetery immediately in front, turn right and at the end of the wooden fence fork right. 25 yards further on fork left onto the path which leads back to the start point.

Barle Valley and Court Down
3½ miles (5.5 kms)

**Start: Public car park adjacent to Exmoor House,
Dulverton, OS map ref: SS913279**

This walk starts at a point where the River Barle rushes through Dulverton before it joins the River Exe two miles further south. Dulverton itself is a thriving community which acts as a link between the southern half of Exmoor and the larger towns of Tiverton in Devon and Taunton in Somerset. Roads of various sizes fan out in all directions from the town and its narrow streets are scenes of great activity at weekends and during the holiday season. It is as well not to bank on hurrying through Dulverton at any time. There is a wide range of shops in the town, accommodation and a Caravan Club site on a bank of the river. If there is time to spare, it is well worth visiting the Exmoor National Park Centre which is in the town centre. This provides an excellent opportunity for learning about life in Dulverton and the surrounding area.

The walk starts from the car park next to the National Park Headquarters, reached by turning off the main road at the Bridge Inn. To begin the walk, return to the Bridge Inn and turn right over the bridge. Turn immediately right again along a road that is the start of paths to Hawkridge and Tarr Steps. Carry straight on up this road, ignoring the left turn, to pass Rose Cottage and The Mount, before a short, steep climb to a signpost by a cottage.

Continue straight ahead and, in a few yards, a gap in the hedge will give a good view of the older part of Dulverton huddled below

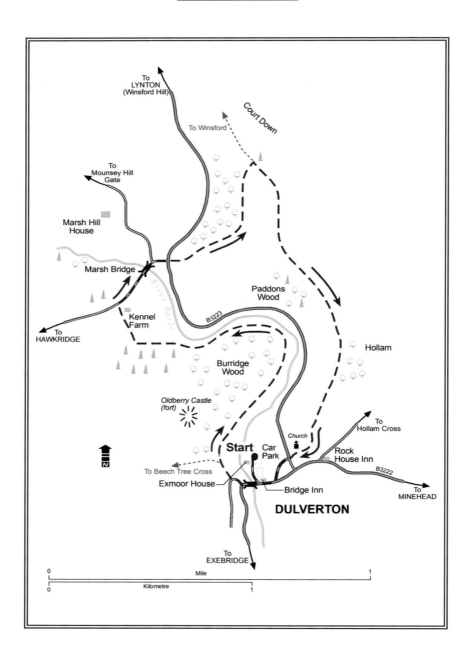

To
LYNTON
(Winsford Hill)

Court Down

To Winsford

To
Mounsey Hill
Gate

Marsh Hill
House

River Barle

Marsh Bridge

Paddons
Wood

Kennel
Farm

B3223

To
HAWKRIDGE

Hollam

Burridge
Wood

Oldberry Castle
(fort)

To
Hollam Cross

N

Church

Rock
House Inn

Start Car
Park

To Beech Tree Cross

B3222

Exmoor House

Bridge Inn

To
MINEHEAD

DULVERTON

To
EXEBRIDGE

0	Mile	1

| 0 | Kilometre | 1 |

26

the church. The track now enters Burridge Wood, which was purchased for public enjoyment through the generosity of Miss B. K. Abbott and Mr Auberon Herbert, late of Dulverton and Pixton respectively. Further along the path is a memorial plaque to mark these gifts.

On the way through the woods there is a good chance of sighting some of the red deer that seem to use this area for cover and feeding nearly all the year round. After passing meadows on the right, the path runs along the river bank and then climbs sharply. This is only a short climb and the path descends to river level again. As the river veers away to your right, the path carries straight on. At a fork, take the right hand path to cross a small stream. In front is Kennel Farm and the path passes between the buildings to the road.

Turn right onto the road and 250 yards further on is Marsh Bridge. Just before crossing the bridge there are some grass covered ruins on the right. These are the remains of a chapel-of-ease erected by Mr Locke of Northmoor in the late 19th century. After crossing Marsh Bridge, turn right and cross over the small footbridge spanning a stream that joins the Barle at this point. Cross the road, and take the short stretch of road up to the higher road. Go straight over this road onto a stony track signposted Court Down. Take great care because there is poor visibility for motorists coming down from Winsford Hill on the left.

Now there is a stony track to follow uphill to the highest point of the walk, ignoring one track that joins from the right. Keep on uphill but do take time to note the remarkable mixture of trees, especially the sweet chestnuts which are comparatively rare in this area. This mixture of trees and vegetation means that there is a wide variety of birds to be spotted and both rabbits and squirrels are plentiful.

The top is finally gained at a T junction. Turn right onto a wide, level track where there is a seat underneath some pine trees. Carry on southwards back towards Dulverton. Soon on the right there is a double gateway with restricted views into the Barle valley and beyond. In the distance to the right are Anstey Commons stretching up to the ridge way that runs from Dulverton. Away to the left the distant views are all in mid-Devon and on a day of good visibility the last range of hills before the coast east of Exeter can be seen.

The path descends steadily now with the dense woods of Paddons and Weir Cleeve on the right. Further on, where the woods of Hollam run on the left, a beautiful carpet of bluebells is to be seen in the late spring. The track rises slightly and then sharply descends to the entrance of the former school. Turn left, and then right down the steps leading past All Saints' church and just before the school gates, the town can be entered past the bank and the Lion Hotel.

The way back to the Bridge Inn is straight on down the street passing the town hall with its double flight of steps. You will find the National Park Centre on the right next to the library. Follow the small alley at the side of the National Park Centre to return to the car park where you started.

Dane's Brook to Castle Bridge
3½ miles (5.5 kms)

Start: Whiterocks Down, OS map ref: SS870291

Two principal features of the southern part of Exmoor are the Rivers Exe and Barle, which rise within 2 miles of each other on the Chains, a high, wet area south of Lynton. They run on parallel courses, first eastwards then south to join below Dulverton. They are short rivers but in this country of high rainfall, varying from 80 inches per year on the Chains to 60 inches at Dulverton, they gather strength very quickly.

On this walk the largest tributary of the Barle will be followed for its last dash through woodlands. This is the Dane's Brook, which starts its life as Litton Water and for its whole length of 8 miles constitutes the boundary between Devon and Somerset. There is an excellent chance of seeing red deer at most times of the year and herds of twenty or more are quite common.

To find the start from Withypool, take the Hawkridge road, and after 2 ½ miles fork left at the first road junction. Ignore the turnings off to the left for Tarr Steps and Hawkridge and carry straight on towards Dulverton. After nearly 5 miles from Withypool, Venford Farm will be passed on the right and 500 yards further on there is a blue-tipped footpath sign on the right, pointing left to Hawkridge and other places. This is the walk start point and there is plenty of parking space on the roadside. Alternatively this point can be reached by taking the Hawkridge road from Dulverton, turning right at Five Cross Ways, and from the junction it is only ¾ mile to the start.

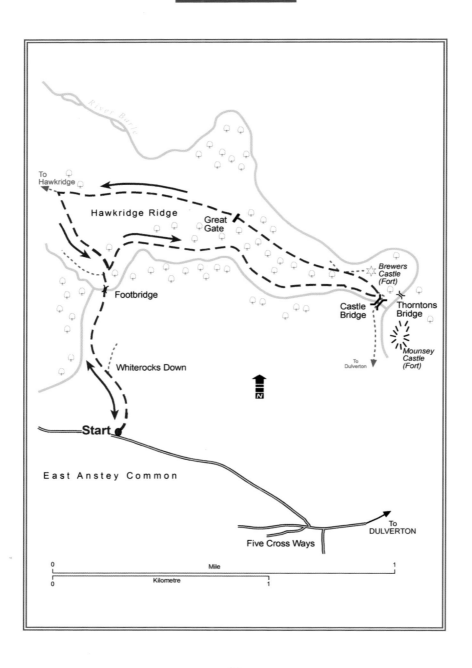

River Burle

To Hawkridge

Hawkridge Ridge

Great Gate

Brewers Castle (Fort)

Footbridge

Castle Bridge

Thorntons Bridge

To Dulverton

Mounsey Castle (Fort)

Whiterocks Down

N

Start

East Anstey Common

Five Cross Ways

To DULVERTON

| 0 | Mile | 1 |
| 0 | Kilometre | 1 |

Go through the gate on the bridleway signed 'Hawkridge'. Cross the first field diagonally to the right, in which can be seen some of the outcrops of white stone that give the area its name of Whiterocks Down. Go through a narrow gateway and then take the path to the left signposted "Bridleway Danesbrook". The path descends gradually to pass through a gap in a beech hedge 300 yards further on.

Carry straight on, still downhill on a well defined stony path. Down to the left can be heard the rush of a stream running down from Venford to the Dane's Brook. After bracken covered slopes, the path goes through another gate, then enters oak woodland and the descent steepens to the footbridge over the Dane's Brook.

Cross the bridge and carry straight on for about 100 yards along a wide track that climbs over a stony stretch to a three-way signpost. Continue straight on for Castle Bridge. The track now follows the river to Castle Bridge and can be boggy in places.

Just before the river joins the Barle, you will reach Castle Bridge. It gets its name from Mounsey Castle on the other side of the Barle and Brewer's Castle, which lies on the slopes above. Although the 'castles' are named after Norman lords, they were in fact constructed for defence in the Iron Age, nearly 2500 years ago.

To continue the walk, do not cross the river but turn sharp left following the sign pointing to Hawkridge. Climb steadily uphill on a wide stony track with views of the River Barle below to the right.

The track leaves the woodland through a gate into open grass-land. Continue on this track along Hawkridge Ridge. Away to the left can be seen the starting point of this walk beside East Anstey Common and behind is the Barle valley with the tree covered Mounsey Castle prominent on the left. Go through a gate, keeping to the vehicle track with a hedge bank to your left. To the right is another view of the Barle valley where it bends sharply downstream from Tarr Steps beside the Hawkridge road.

Pass through another gate keeping to the track. In another 200 yards a gate is reached with a three way signpost. Here, leave the track, following the bridleway for East Anstey across the field. Pass through a gate behind some gorse, and then follow the blue waymarks downhill, turning right at a fence before continuing steeply down on a stony section.

This rejoins the outward route at the signpost near the bridge across the Dane's Brook.. At the signpost turn right to retrace the first part of the walk across the bridge and up onto Whiterocks Down with the assistance of blue waymarks to refresh the memory.

Tarr Steps to Anstey Gate and Hawkridge
7 ½ miles or 2 ½ miles (12 kms or 4 kms)

Start: Tarr Steps car park,
OS map ref: SS873324

The longer of these walks from Tarr Steps covers much of the landscape for which Exmoor is famous. There are river valleys, woodland, cultivated farmland, rough grazing and open moorland to be traversed during the course of this walk.

To reach Tarr Steps take the Exford-Dulverton road to Winsford Hill and follow the road signs from there, passing through Liscombe before turning into the large car park (please note, there is a parking fee). Take the path that runs downhill parallel to the road, to Tarr Steps, passing Tarr Farm on the right. Cross the clapper bridge; this has spanned the River Barle for at least 500 years.

Once over, fork right up a drive signed as a bridleway to Withypool Hill. The house up here was originally Hawkridge rectory, and later a hotel. After 100 yards, fork right onto a steep stony track. Continue up, passing through a gateway, before turning right into a sunken section. At the next gateway, do not go through it, but turn left up the field, keeping the hedge to your right. At the next gate, pause for breath and look back for grand views of Ashway Side and the summit of Winsford Hill.

Go through this gate and walk beside the hedge on the left, through the next gate and on to another. Here go straight on, following the footpath through Parsonage Farm. The yellow waymarks take you past the farm buildings, before following the drive as it descends and then turns left over a stream. It then climbs

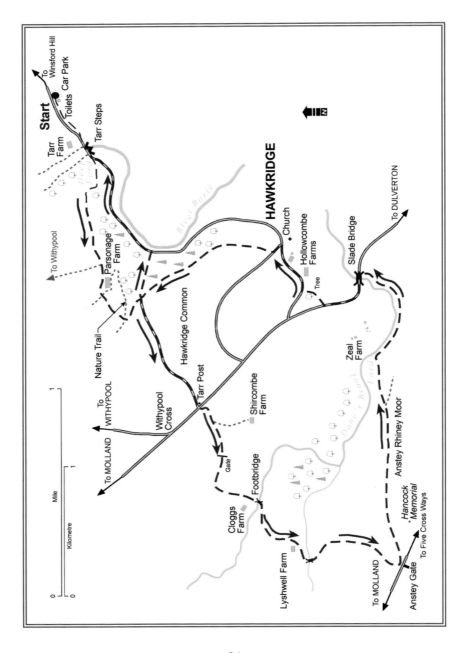

again to reach a footpath sign at the end of a metalled road.

If the shorter walk is being tackled, turn left here down the Restricted Byway signed "Penny Bridge", and then turn left on the road back to Tarr Steps. If you are doing the longer walk, turn right and follow the road uphill, passing Huntercombe on your right. On reaching the road junction at Tarr Post turn left, then after 35 yards turn right through the gate down the drive to Shircombe Farm.

On the horizon can be seen Molland Moor on the right and West Anstey Common to the left. This walk is heading for Anstey Gate, which is at the top of the hedge between the two commons. Follow the farm track to the next set of gates. Do not go straight on, but turn right onto a bridleway, keeping the hedge to your left.

After 100 yards, pass through a gateway in the hedgebank. Turn immediately right, to follow the hedgebank and blue waymarks to the side of a small valley beside Cloggs Farm. Follow the path down the field, keeping the valley to your right. At its junction with the Dane's Brook, there is a substantial footbridge.

Cross the bridge, turn right and climb diagonally up the track between birch trees. When a low bank is met, follow this up to the gateway in the top hedge. Go through this gate and ahead to the brow of the hill, passing Lyshwell Farm on your right. Turn right after passing the generator buildings and then follow the farm track up to Anstey Gate, crossing a cattle grid onto open moorland.

On arrival at Anstey Gate, turn left across the cattle grid, and in front to the left of the road can be seen the Froude Hancock stone, erected by his friends in memory of a renowned stag hunting gentleman who died in 1933. The route to follow now is across Anstey Rhiney Moor towards Zeal Farm.

Start off half left from the cattle grid on a well used track, which gradually becomes less distinct as it descends away from the road. However, you can just see the tops of the buildings above the trees of Zeal Farm some distance in front of you on the left had side of the moor to assist in keeping to the correct lines across this open moorland. This is easy downhill walking and, once the road is left behind, there is a good chance of sighting red deer. Over to the left below Shircombe Farm can be seen Shircombe Brake and the wild valley of the Dane's Brook.

Keep going in the same direction gradually descending to the river that runs down the valley below Zeal Farm. The path eventually becomes a gully as it goes down through the gorse before emerging at the river (Zeal Ford) with a fingerpost on the bank. Turn right here for Slade Bridge, following a permitted path that picks its way through woods with the river down below. Avoid descending to the river, but keep higher to emerge onto a road. Turn left on the road and Slade Bridge is approx 50 metres further down.

Continue over the bridge and follow the road as it climbs steeply past the entrance to Zeal Farm. On the next bend, turn off right through a gate, following a bridleway sign for Hawkridge. Climb away from the gate, and then head for the tree surrounded by railings in the middle of the field. Turn half left, and head for the gate in the top corner of the field. Go through the gate onto the road and turn right into Hawkridge.

At the village centre turn left on the road to Withypool and then, after the post box, turn right through a small gate signed to Tarr Steps. Pass through a narrow gate, and follow the path over a stile into a field. Follow the direction indicated by the signpost for Tarr Steps to cross three fields before climbing a stile in a field corner. Keep to the left of the hedge and follow the path, which passes through another two gateways to reach the Parsonage Farm entrance road.

Turn right down the 'Hardway', signposted "Restricted Byway Penny Bridge" and descend steeply between oak trees on the left and conifers on the right to meet the road from Hawkridge at Penny Bridge. Turn left onto this little used road and follow it alongside the Barle back to Tarr Steps. On crossing the clapper bridge, retrace your route back to the car park.

Winsford Hill
5½ miles (9 kms)

Start: Winsford village car park, OS map ref: SS906349

Winsford has the reputation of being one of the most beautiful villages in England and the residents try very hard to justify this reputation. It is also known as the 'village of bridges', with eight bridges of various sizes crossing the River Exe and the Winn Brook. In the centre there is plenty of evidence that the art of thatching is still not lost in Somerset. It is also the birth-place of Ernest Bevin, the wartime Minister of Labour who lent his name to the 'Bevin Boys' who were conscripted to work in the mines. Later Bevin became an eminent Foreign Secretary.

The village is easy to find on the wide road leaving the A369 at Coppleham Cross, just north of Bridgetown. There is ample parking space in the village car park opposite the garage. To start the walk, go past Bridge Cottage towards the War Memorial and turn right over the bridge beside the ford. Walk on up Ash Lane, passing Winsford Church, with its lofty square tower nearly 100 feet high and modern houses on the right hand side. Just after the last of these there is a footpath sign on the left pointing the way to Winsford Hill via the Punchbowl. Take this path, which is confirmed with yellow waymarks. After passing in front of the new house, the path takes a fairly level course through several fields. Be sure to use the gates that are waymarked.

The stream down to the left is the Winn Brook, from which Winsford derives its name. The wood climbing up behind it is Burrow Wood. Eventually the path joins the entrance road to

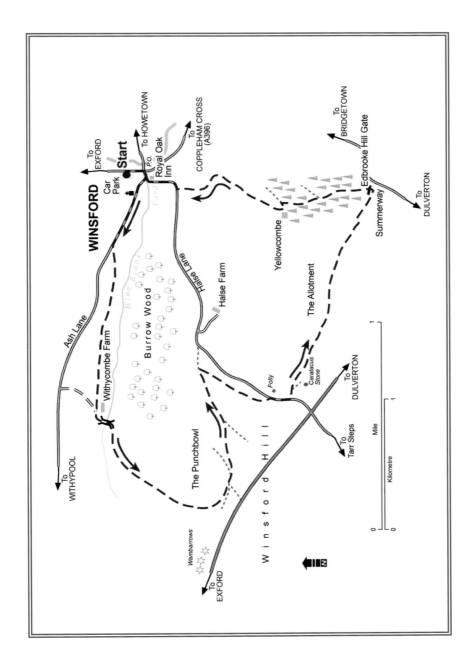

Withycombe Farm (a very common name for farms on Exmoor). To the left at this point, there is a fine view into the heart of the Punchbowl. The path will follow the rim of this natural phenomenon.

Go round the right hand edge of the farm building, following the blue waymarks. Cross the wooden bridge over the stream, climb up a short stretch of concrete road and then turn sharp right to go through the gate on the left. It is a steady climb now up to the highest point of the Punchbowl rim and it is well worth several pauses to look back at Winsford nestling in the Exe valley with the Brendon Hills in the background.

A gate on your right, near the top of the rise, leads into a field and has a bridleway sign pointing the way up the hill. Go through the gate and head left going uphill with the hedge bank on your left until you come to another gate. This gate leads out onto the wide open spaces of Winsford Hill. Continue straight on uphill on a wide grassy track. To the right, beyond Great Ash Farm, can be seen the steep banks of the Exe valley below Exford and behind to the left can be seen Dunkery Beacon.

The path steadily veers to the left, getting nearer to the edge of the Punchbowl. At the highest point there are paths joining from the right and here the blue waymarking ceases. From here it is possible to make a short diversion by turning right up to the three Wambarrows, which crown Winsford Hill at its highest point of 1399 ft. These are just three of the 300 or more barrows, or burial mounds, within Exmoor National Park that are relics of the late Bronze Age, lasting between 1600 BC and 500 BC.

To continue the walk, return to the top edge of the Punchbowl and carry on round the edge for another 100 yards until you are halfway round and then fork slightly right on a well used track. Slightly to the left on the horizon in front can be seen the telecommunications mast on top of the Brendon Hills at Goosemoor.

After about ½ mile another path joins from behind, and the path in front forks. Go straight ahead, taking the right hand fork and follow the track as it winds down towards the road. As the track approaches the road, a house called 'Folly' appears across the road on the left handside. Join the road opposite Folly house, follow it for 200 yards and then turn sharp left as instructed by a footpath sign to Winsford.

After 50 yards go through a gate and then turn half right to cross The Allotment. If it is wished to take the opportunity of visiting the Caratacus Stone, it lies about 300 yards up the path to the right before passing through the gate. It will be found semi-concealed in the gorse to the right hand side. This stone is of great historical interest because it is the only inscribed one of its age in Somerset. It is believed to have been a guide or sighting stone before it was inscribed CARATACI NEPVS (kinsman of Caratacus) in the 5th or 6th century to commemorate a notable person. It suffered its first vandalism in 1890, when the corner with the letter N on it was broken off with a pick. This fragment was found in 1906, when the present shelter was erected, and fixed back on the next year. The whole stone was again vandalised in 1936 when it was dug out of the ground (all 7cwt of it!), probably to satisfy local curiosity concerning the possibility of buried treasure beneath. In 1937 it was re-erected and has been successfully protected since then.

The path across the heather covered Allotment is level and nearly straight for a mile. This is a regular haunt for lapwing, curlew, skylarks and of course the ever present meadow pipits. As the conifers of Yellowcombe come into sight in front, the path gradually descends to pass through a small gate into Summerway.

Carry on in the same direction towards a disused pit on the left hand side of the field. Above this pit is a signpost that indicates that the path to Winsford is left through Edbrooke Hill Gate along a wide forestry track. Now the path descends rapidly through the plantation. Very often rabbits can be seen scurrying around here and occasionally the cry of a cock pheasant can surprise when all else is quiet.

With Yellowcombe Cottage below to the left, the track forks. Take the left track leading down to a bridge. Cross the bridge and turn right. There is a steady pull up a sunken lane with overgrown hedges on both sides and occasionally, deep mud underfoot. This path carries on climbing and then swings left to give a bird's eye view of all Winsford down below and Howetown away to the right. It is a steep downhill path now, on bare rock in places, to join the road into Winsford from Winsford Hill. Turn right onto this road, passing the Karslake House Hotel and the Royal Oak Inn en route for the car park.

The Exe Valley
6½ miles (10.5 kms)

Start: Exford car park, OS map ref: SS854384

Exford is near the geographical centre of Exmoor, and if Exmoor is 'the land of the horse', Exford can be considered its capital. There are two hotels, both with extensive blocks of stables and plenty of other stabling in the village, which has been home of the Devon and Somerset Stag Hounds. Exford is easily found on the B3224/B3223 between Wheddon Cross and Simonsbath and the car park entrance is opposite the Crown Hotel in the village centre.

Starting from the back of the car park, walk past the National Park Depot and through a kissing gate by a screen of rhododendrons. Keep to the river bank through the next two fields. Turn right to cross the Exe river and follow bridleway signs to Room Hill through the buildings of Court Farm, turning left, right and then left again to go through a gate into a lane on the side of a field. Follow this sunken lane upwards, go through a gate into a corridor with a hedge on one side and fencing on the other. The path curves round to the right encountering another gate at the end of the track. Turn left at this gate to continue on an enclosed track.

Go through a hunting gate, across a stream and then climb up a steep stony track with open hillside on the right and a small wood on the left. As the climb eases, the track enters an open field. Looking to the left, the outskirts of Exford can be seen with the church in the background. To the right of the church is a property called Stone with the Rowbarrows on the horizon behind and

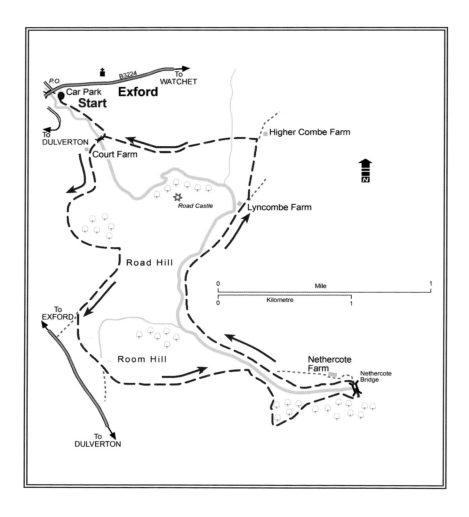

Dunkery Beacon to the right. Half left, in the corner of a field below, can be seen the remaining earthworks of Road Castle, an Iron Age fort overlooking the river.

Keep straight on to a gate on the other side of the field, go through the gate and then turn right, climbing up again on Road Hill. Walk by the hedge on the right, as directed by the bridleway sign. Where the hedge bears round to the left, carry straight on through the next two fields. After the second gate and to the left, there is a wild combe tumbling down from Room Hill to the Exe. Keep going straight ahead from this second gate through another gate into fields until you reach a small three way bridleway sign. At the sign fork left round the head of the combe. Then the path goes in a southerly direction between gorse bushes up to a signpost to Winsford. Follow the sign, sweeping left around a fence surrounding the head of a marshy combe.

Continue along this path in a south easterly direction then, on reaching the hedge, bear left towards Nethercote Farm. The last part of this descent is a steep, well worn track which goes down to the river. Turn right and follow the riverbank downstream, going through a gate on the right by the ford and following yellow waymarks to Nethercote Bridge.

For the next two miles of riverside walking, there is a good chance of seeing dippers and herons and possibly mink and kingfishers. Go through the hunting gate and out onto the farm access road at Nethercote Bridge. Cross the bridge and then turn left through the first gateway indicated by the "permitted path to Exford" sign. On this section the path follows a route which has been negotiated to avoid inconveniencing the farm residents. Follow the river bank through three fields and then turn half right to cross the next field diagonally. Pass through a gate and carry straight on, crossing the track down to the ford.

After passing the two small huts high above the track on the right, which are not observation posts but merely pump houses for water supplies, there are no signs of human habitation along this beautiful open valley walk. After a while the path curves up to meet an old stone lane which winds along the top of the cleave before entering two grass fields and coming to Lyncombe Farm. Just before the farm on the left hand side is a very well preserved pack horse bridge leading up to the field below Road Castle. Unfortunately there is no public right of way over this bridge.

Go straight through the farmyard and up along the farm entrance road. Ignore the yellow waymarked route to the left and keep following the bridleway along the track. Fork left at the next junction and then climb gradually to Higher Combe Farm. Turn left just before this farm following the public footpath signs for Exford and head down to the bridge at the bottom of the field. Cross the bridge and stile and climb up out of the combe.

Walk across the middle of the field and also the next one, and then follow the hedge on the right to the next gateway. Go through the gate and follow the track down to Court Farm. Turn right just before the bridge and retrace the first part of the walk along the river bank.

Withypool Common and Barle Valley
3 miles (5 kms)

Start: Withypool village car park, OS map ref: SS844354

Withypool is a compact, attractive village that has been established at this important river crossing for a very long time. The present road bridge is the first one north of Dulverton capable of carrying heavy traffic across the River Barle. R.D.Blackmore, the author of *Lorna Doone*, frequently stayed here and there is an original letter of his, reserving accommodation, on the wall inside the Royal Oak.

Withypool is an ideal walking centre with a wide variety of walks fanning out in all directions. It is adjacent to the wide open spaces of Winsford Hill to the south east and Withypool Common to the south west. The walk described below is wet in places, and crosses uneven ground, so good footwear is a necessity.

The village is clearly signposted from Exford, only 3 miles away. From Dulverton, take the B3223 over Winsford Hill, turning left 8 miles from Dulverton. To find the starting point, drive over the bridge opposite the post office and the car park is on the right hand side.

Start the walk by turning right out of the car park and right again on the Sandyway road. About 600 yards up the road, immediately after the entrance to Waterhouse Farm, fork right onto a path signposted to Landacre. Follow the vehicle track straight across Waterhouse Common towards a large tree in the corner of the field in front. After the tree, the track bends to the right. Ignoring the gateway, continue to follow the hedge line, keeping it to your right.

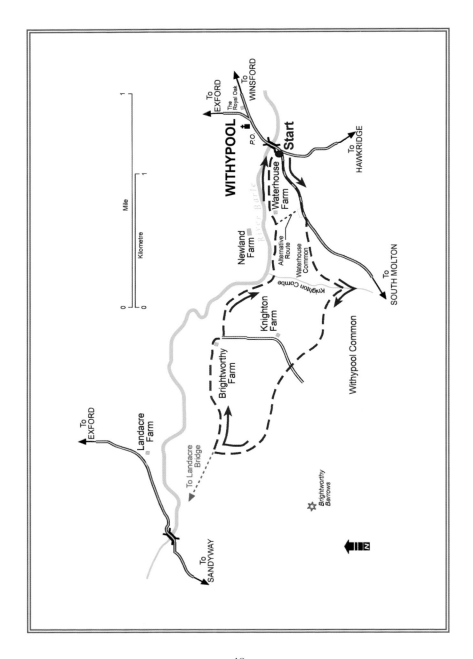

Pass through a wet area of rushes before the path narrows and enters high gorse.

Follow this as it descends towards the bottom of Knighton Combe. As you approach the bottom, look out for a narrow track that branches off left into the gorse, just before you reach a clump of five beech trees in the bank to your right. Turn left along this path, heading for the bottom of the diagonal gully opposite.

Cross the stream, and climb up out of the combe in the steep gully, bearing right. On reaching the hedge, turn left and follow it to cross a tarmac drive. Up in front can be seen Brightworthy Barrows, at 1404 feet.

Continue to follow the line of the hedge. On the open moor to the left there are usually Exmoor Horn and Scottish Blackface sheep. After crossing a small stream, the hedge curves away to the right, while the path rises a little more steeply to carve its way through a boggy stretch.

The wall comes back in from the right as the top is reached, and then a gradual descent is started. Historic Landacre Bridge appears down in the valley below. When Exmoor was a Royal Forest this was an important place, as courts known as Swainmotes were held here. Payments for grazing were collected, and Forest Law was administered. Now the bridge over the Barle is a very popular beauty spot, and on a sunny Sunday afternoon there will be many visitors here.

To follow this walk, do not make towards the bridge but keep to the boundary hedge, avoiding some boggy patches, heading down until a footpath sign is reached. Turn right through the gate, sign-posted to Withypool, and follow a sunken track leading all the way to Brightworthy Farm. Shortly before reaching the farm, the path goes over a stile through the hedge on the left and then across a small bridge. This path follows the field edge, before crossing over a stile. Turn left to follow the yellow waymarking, keeping the farm buildings on your right. On passing through the gate out of the farm, head straight across the next field, to pass through a hedge-bank and down to the river.

Just before this path reaches the river bank, turn right and then follow the path near the river bank. Although this is usually wet, it is a most attractive stretch of path along the Barle and the worst of the mud can usually be avoided. Along this path there are several stiles and footbridges, including a clapper bridge and a boardwalk. Eventually the path reaches a "private land" sign and there is a signpost pointing left and right. Here there is a choice of routes.

One route is to turn right through a gate, signposted Withypool Hill, and up a stony track leading to Waterhouse Common. On crossing the stile at the top, turn left and go back down the road to the car park. Alternatively turn left, signposted Withypool, and cross over the stile. Make for the left hand corner of the large building in front, which is an indoor riding school, and then pass through the next gate to reach a stile leading onto a green lane. Go straight on and through a hunting gate to return to the river bank again, crossing over another stile to Withypool Bridge and the car park.

Cow Castle
6½ miles (10.5 kms)

Start: Birchcleave Wood, Simonsbath, OS map ref: SS774393

Anybody who has travelled through Exmoor could be forgiven for expecting something different when they first arrive at Simonsbath. All roads seem to be signposted to the village from many miles away but the visitor can pass through in seconds without realising he has seen all there is to be seen. It is the highest village, in the largest parish with one of the smallest populations on Exmoor!

Up to the early 19th century, there was only one building here and this is now the Simonsbath House Hotel. Originally it was the residence of the Warden who was responsible for the administration of the Royal Forest of Exmoor. 'Forest' did not here mean a densely wooded area but country where game was preserved for hunting. In fact when a survey of Exmoor was made in 1814, the surveyor reported that there were only 37 trees in the moor, all growing around the Warden's lodge. He missed one which will be encountered on a later walk - the Hoar Oak.

In 1818 it was decided to dispose of the Royal Forest in lots, and tenders were invited. The successful purchaser of the most lots was a Mr John Knight from Worcester who paid £50,000 for 10,000 acres. This gentleman and his son Frederic endeavoured to create a farming and industrial community in the area, based on a new village built at Simonsbath. The full story of the 'reclamation' of Exmoor Forest is a fascinating saga and there are several informative books on the subject. Simonsbath lies 5 miles from Exford on the B3223 road to Lynton and 5 miles east of Challacombe on the

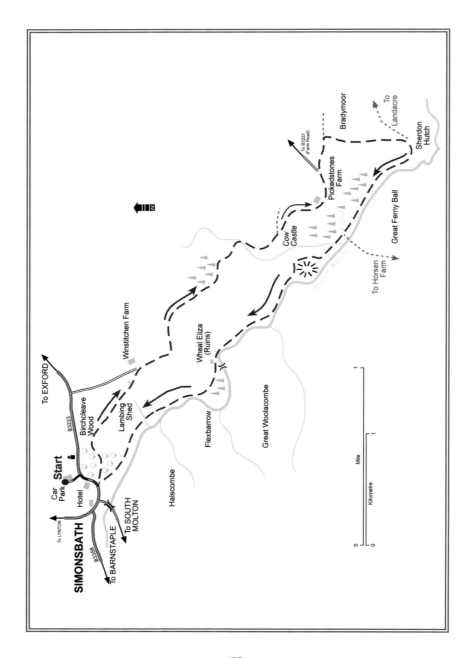

B3358 road. A car park together with toilets and a picnic area are down a turning opposite Birchcleave Wood.

Walk back to the road and turn right to pass Exmoor Forest Hotel. Cross the road by Pound Cottage, entering Birchcleave Wood at the signpost opposite. A little way into the wood there is a signpost. The first half of this walk follows the blue waymarked path to Pickedstones, so begin by climbing through mature beeches planted by the Knights in 1840. At an altitude of 1300 feet, this is the highest known beech wood in the country.

At the top of the wood turn left and walk about 250 yards to a gate on the right. Go through and follow the hedge to the next gate. Go through this and then the one in front to enter a field with a pond to your left. Now follow the bank on the right to the second gate. Turn left after going through this gate and follow a hedge down through two fields to a small lambing shed. Away to the right can be seen the heights of Halscombe and Great Woolcombe towering above the Barle valley.

Go through the hunting gate opposite the shed door and turn half left to follow a fence to reach the end of a tarmac road by Winstitchen Farm. Turn right by the gate and walk by a stone faced bank to reach a gate on the left. Go through this and follow the hedge on the left through two fields to a small plantation of conifers. Straight ahead can be seen the cairn of Brightworthy Barrows beyond the buildings of Pickedstones Farm.

Continue to follow the hedge, veering left round the edge of the plantation. This descends to meet a small track at the head of a valley. Turn left, and then curve around the top of this valley to join a track that runs down its left side. This drops to a bridge over White Water. Turn right after passing through a gate on the other side and climb up the track to Pickedstones Farm. To the right is

Cow Castle, an Iron Age defensive fort and to its left is the rocky outcrop known as the Calf.

Continue upwards with a wire fence on the right and, as the path levels out, go through two gates, crossing small streams between them. Follow the bank on the left and 200 yards further on turn left through a gate, passing the Pickedstones farmhouse and stables on the left. Take the road straight ahead going uphill and after passing through a gateway turn right through a gate at the blue waymarked sign for Landacre.

Follow the hedge on the right, veering slightly left at the end of the field to go through a gate out into the open expance of Bradymoor. The three hills of similar shape in front from right to left are Brightworthy, Withypool and Winsford Hills, all crowned with round barrows.

Turn right, and follow the boundary bank downhill until you meet a track which passes through a gate. The way back now follows the blue waymarked bridleway to "Simonsbath". Go through this gate and continue on a pleasant steady descent to another gate into a large conifer plantation. Cow Castle now appears ahead. Carry on through the wood and, when the track arrives at Horsen Ford, turn right towards the footbridge.

This is as good a place as any in which to take that overdue break for refreshment. More than half the walk has been completed and it is now a riverside walk nearly all the way back to Simonsbath. Press on upstream, keeping on the east side of the river and crossing White Water by the footbridge. Keep to the right around the base of Cow Castle and go through a hunting gate adjacent to a river barrier. Continue along the bank to a row of beech trees. Go through the bank before the first tree and follow the path to the other end of the trees. Pass through the trees and turn right along the bank.

After the path has passed beneath a rocky outcrop, there is a wire fence on the left hand side, follow the fence, looking out for stonechats in one of their favourite haunts. Just before the next hedge, climb up through wild raspberries to go through a hunting gate. Down below are the remains of Wheal Eliza mine and, in front, the ruins of the miners' cottages. This is all there is to be seen of another venture of the Knight family when they mined for iron ore on the site of a former copper mine.

After passing the cottages take the path to the right of the large natural mound in front, known as Flexbarrow. The river is soon in sight again and now the path hugs a steep hillside. Looking upstream, Simonsbath comes into sight round the edge of Birchcleave Wood. After passing through one hunting gate, there is a sunken track which leads to another hunting gate into the wood and in a few minutes the starting point is reached.

Pinkery Pond and Chains Barrow
4 miles (6.5 kms)

Start: Pinkery car park, OS map ref: SS728402

Travelling between Simonsbath and Challacombe, the road follows one of the original tracks built by the Knight family in the early 19th century when they were reclaiming the old Royal Forest. This particular road was very important for the carriage of lime from North Devon ports, lime being essential to sweeten the sour moorland.

The high ground to the north is known as the Chains and claims an average rainfall of 80 inches per year. Most of the principal rivers in Exmoor originate from this peaty mass: the Barle and Exe running south to the English Channel, and Farley Water, Hoaroak Water, and West Lyn running north into the Bristol Channel. Providing that some care is used, it is possible to walk this route without getting wet feet, but good footwear is recommended. It is also a very exposed walk, so it is best to wait for a fine day with good visibility.

To find the starting point, drive west from Simonsbath on the B3358 towards Challacombe for 3 miles. Park the car in the first roadside parking area on the right after the entrance to Driver Farm. Alternatively drive 2 miles east from Challacombe, and the car park required is the second on the left after the entrance to Pinkery Outdoor Education Centre.

Start by walking on the wide verge towards Challacombe. The wild combe opposite the starting point leads up to a mysterious place known as Mole's Chamber. Here was once a very isolated inn,

the Acland Arms, which was used by the miners who endeavoured to extract iron ore from this area. After passing through another parking area, you will see the gateway to the drive to the Pinkery Centre on the right.

This estate was purchased by Exmoor National Park Authority in 1970 with the aid of a government grant. There had been a public outcry concerning proposals to plant conifer forests on the Chains in 1957. The whole of the estate is still farmed and Pinkery farm buildings have been developed into a renowned Outdoor Education Centre, principally for the use of school children.

Walk up the drive to the Centre with the infant River Barle on the left. Just before the buildings, fork left onto the yellow waymarked footpath. Go through one gateway and veer right to go through a gap in the bank. Above you is a wind turbine that generates much of the power needed at the Pinkery Centre. Bear to the left of the turbine, gradually drawing closer to the river again. Go through a narrow gate and follow the path which runs parallel with the river. Keep to the higher path and follow this to the beginning of the River Barle in the face of the retaining dam for Pinkery Pond.

This damming up of the source of the Barle was yet another of the Knight family projects. It is not definitely known why this was undertaken and there are various theories which have backing by different historians. The most widely held is that the reservoir of water created was to be used for topping up a 'canal' system over the Chains to provide water to drive farm machinery or pump water from the mines. Another is that it was to provide water as ballast for an incline railway bringing iron ore out of the Barle valley to be carried over the moors to the sea by rail. Others believe that it was the basis of an irrigation system and a lower 'canal' certainly seems to end as a system of 'field gutters' for this purpose.

On passing through the gate at the top of the dam turn right towards Exe Head. The path is traversing the Chains, and it was from here that the disastrous Lynmouth flood in 1952 originated. The moor was already saturated from a wet August and then a phenomenal thunderstorm sluiced off the waterlogged peat to cause unprecedented flooding both to the north and south.

This next section of path can be wet, so take your time, following the wall bank to your right. After 400 yards two gates are reached. Pass through the second one, as the ground is much easier on the other side, and continue to follow the line of the wall bank.

It is now a steady walk to reach a signpost and gate to your left. In fine weather, it is worth passing through the gate and following the finger that points to Chains Barrow. While not visible from the gate, in a very short while the barrow will be seen in the distance, topped by a trig point.

This is one of the best moorland viewpoints on Exmoor. Looking east over Long Chains Combe and Brendon Common, Dunkery Beacon is the hill on the skyline. To the south, Five Barrows can clearly be seen breaking the skyline and to the west there are long distance views into north and mid-Devon. With good visibility it is possible to spot the height of Brown Willy on Bodmin Moor in Cornwall.

Retrace the path back to the signpost and go back through the gate in the wall. Walk across the field in the general direction of the sign pointing to the B3358 road - there are blue waymarked posts to help you keep straight. Unfortunately these posts are also used as rubbing posts by cattle and sheep with the inevitable result that there is rarely a complete set.

This is a gradual descent through a very large field but as long as the markers are followed, there are easy walking conditions, Go through the gate on the far side, turn left and follow the hedge boundary on the left through two fields back down to the road and car park.

Bossington Hill and Hurlstone
3 miles (5 kms)

Start: Bossington Hill car park,
OS map ref: SS911477

Minehead may not be strictly part of Exmoor, but its claim as a 'gateway' to Exmoor National Park can certainly be justified. On its doorstep lies North Hill; not only a beautiful area to traverse by car and explore on foot, but it provides the most perfect viewpoint for the northeast of Exmoor.

This walk starts from the car park at the extreme western end of the scenic road, which runs the length of North Hill. To find this road from the centre of Minehead, travel down the parade towards the sea and turn left opposite W.H. Smith's. Take the first turning on the left, and follow the signposts to North Hill, passing below the magnificent church and through Higher Town. To the right is the Bristol Channel stretching back to Weston-super-Mare and beyond, with the squat islands of Flat Holm and Steep Holm in the middle distance. On the other side of the channel is Wales, with views all the way into the Brecon Beacons on clear days. Straight behind are the Quantock Hills and to the left is the rest of Exmoor.

The tarmac finally ends at the loose stone of a car park. Turn right into the portion which faces the sea. The start of the walk is at the road-ward end of this car park, where a track goes off through a vehicle barrier. Follow this path off from the car park. Over to the left, a cairn marks the top of Bossington Hill. Down below to the left is Bossington Beach with its wide variety of bird life and at the far

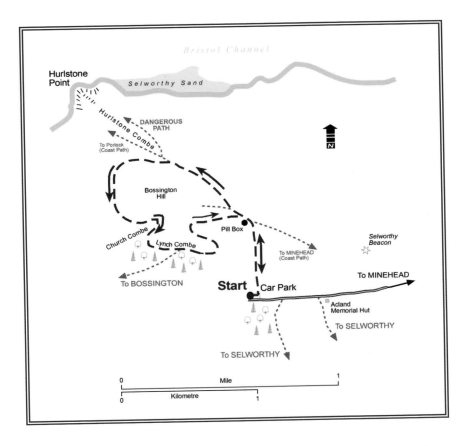

end of the beach nestles Porlock Weir with Ashley Combe and then Culbone Woods behind. After this the wooded 'hogsback' cliffs stretch away westward to Foreland Point.

Keep to the wide track that bends slightly left by a wartime relic, a concrete pillbox, now grown over and difficult to spot. Down to the left can be seen the sprawl of Porlock in the centre of the fertile vale. At a T-junction turn left, to join the South West Coast. This is the longest of our National Trails, which stretches over 600 miles from Minehead to Poole in Dorset.

Further along the path fork right and, keeping to the Coast Path, head downwards to the top of Hurlstone Combe. With good visibility, there is a fine view of the near part of the Welsh coast stretching from Port Eynon Point in the west to Lavernock Point in the east. Fork left at the top of the combe, leaving the Coast Path, which goes on down the combe itself.

The next stretch is a most impressive, narrow path around the seaward face of Bossington Hill on the 650 foot contour. Nearly straight down below are the paths leading to the former coastguard lookout and the beach. When Porlock comes into view you can look along the shingle ridge to the breach that allows sea water to flood the marsh. Then the picturesque village of Bossington, followed by the hamlet of Lynch, appear. There are several seats along this path where you can pause and enjoy the view.

As the path sweeps inland the next village below in front is Allerford with its well known pack horse bridge, and on the horizon in front is Dunkery Beacon with the cairns Robin How and Joaney How on the hill to the left. The path continues around Church Combe, towards Porlock again, and then into the evergreen holm oak trees of Lynch Combe. Turn left in the combe, following the footpath sign to Minehead. There now follows a steady climb homewards.

Halfway up the slope a T junction is reached. The right hand path, signed to Selworthy Woods is a shorter route back to the car park but is a steep climb. At the top of this steep short cut turn right and follow the path along to the car park. For those with more time, and little inclination to struggle up steep hills, the left hand route is a more gentle way back. Start heading towards the top of Bossington Hill, still following the bridleway for Selworthy Beacon signs, then turn right as soon as the cairn appears in front.

Forking off right again when a wide track is reached, the outward path and Coast Path is rejoined. Fork off right again, and bearing right again shortly afterwards returns you to the car park.

To Dunkery Beacon from the East
6 miles (9.5 kms)

Start: Brockwell, nr. Wootton Courtenay,
OS map ref: SS928432

One of Exmoor's greatest assets is the widespread land ownership by the National Trust. There is public access to the open moorland and most of the woodland owned by them, and this is seen to its very best advantage on the 12,000 acre Holnicote Estate. The largest part of this estate was given to the National Trust by Sir Richard Acland in 1944 and together with the other gifts of moorland made by Colonel Walter Wiggin and Mrs Allan Hughes, covers an area from Selworthy Beacon in the north to Dunkery Gate in the south, and from Alderman's Barrow in the west to Brockwell in the east.

This walk, and the four that follow it, are all contained within the estate. There are so many paths and bridleways, it would be possible to walk for a fortnight or more on different routes, and many of the paths are still known by the names given to them by the Acland family. Because of the views, particularly from the top of Dunkery Beacon, it would be as well to pick a fine day with good visibility.

To find the start point, drive to Wootton Courtenay from the A396, Dunster to Tiverton road, leaving it at a point just north of Timberscombe. Go past the village shops and just after passing the Dunkery Hotel on the right, turn left down a dead end road signposted to Brockwell and Ford. Where the road to Ford swings off to the left, there is a National Trust sign and a two-way signpost. Park further along the road, on the left hand side before returning

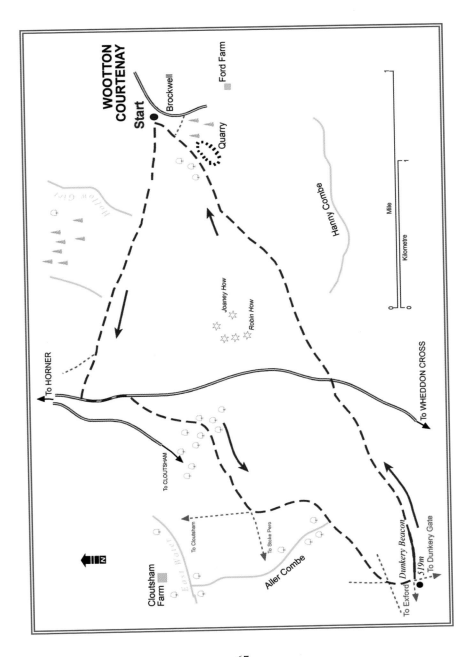

WOOTTON COURTENAY

Start

Brockwell

Ford Farm

Quarry

Hollow Girt

Hanny Combe

Joaney How

Robin How

To HORNER

To WHEDDON CROSS

To CLOUTSHAM

Cloutsham Farm

East Water

To Cloutsham

To Stoke Pero

Aller Combe

Dunkery Beacon

519m

To Dunkery Gate

To Exford

N

Mile

Kilometre

to the signpost.

Follow the level bridleway signed "Luccombe and Dunkery". At the junction take the left fork following the Permitted Bridleway signs towards Webbers Post. There is a narrow uphill stony path at the start but this soon comes out onto the open hillside. Keep following the track as it climbs slowly in a general westerly direction. After a while the path joins another well used track called the Dunkery Path. Turn right following the signs for Webber's Post. Above to the left are first Joaney How and then Robin How, both barrow-topped hills.

Away to the right is Porlock Vale, with Selworthy Beacon above the unmistakable white of Selworthy church. As the path skirts around the top of a depression called Hollow Girt, the compact farm to the right is Holt Ball and further on to the right is the attractive village of Luccombe surrounding its 15th century church. With conifer woods down to the right and Ley Hill appearing in front, it is a steady climb now to skirt the top of Wychanger Combe. Carry straight on, and do not veer off to Webber's Post.

When the path strikes the Dunkery road, turn left, walk up the road for about 300 yards and then, just after the second sharp bend on the road, turn right along a path signposted 'Dicky's Path to Stoke Ridge'. Down to the right is the magnificent Horner valley, with Horner Water curling round Ley Hill and joining up with East Water below Webber's Post. Away up in front is the cairn of Dunkery Beacon; the next objective.

The path plunges down into a wooded combe and climbs out the other side. As the path comes out of the trees, the splendid farmhouse over to the right with its unusual balcony is Cloutsham Farm. Opposite the view of the farmhouse and next to a small rowan tree, the path crosses another grassy track making a small crossroads. Turn left here towards the left of Dunkery Beacon, starting off on a short grassy stretch that soon changes to a narrow stony path.

The path bears right around the head of Aller Combe and then heads for the cairn that can be seen from this point. On reaching the summit it will be seen that the cairn commemorates the handing over of Dunkery Beacon to the National Trust. This hill at the highest point in Exmoor has been used as a beacon for hundreds of years, first to warn of danger and more recently to celebrate royal weddings and jubilees. The all round views are too numerous to mention and it is best to check with the viewpoint indicator adjacent to the cairn.

To set off on the return trip, head eastward (you can check directions from the viewpoint indicator) along a wide track leading towards Brent Knoll - 27 miles away! This is the hill adjacent to the service area on the M5 between Bristol and Taunton. On reaching the road, go straight across on the bridleway signed "Brockwell 1 ¼", and the path can be seen out in front running to the right of Robin and Joaney How. Away to the right are the Brendon Hills beyond Wheddon Cross. The large, deep combe to the right is Hanny Combe, cut by a tributary of the River Avill, which passes through Timberscombe and Dunster.

Keep going down this track enjoying the slow and steady descent. About halfway down there are some hunting paths veering off to the left. Ignore these paths and keep to the main track which curves slightly to the right. The village of Wootton Courtenay should be visible for most of the descent, and acts as a good landmark for which you should aim.

Eventually the path leaves the moor and heads into woodland passing by a signpost showing a path to the right (Mick's Path) and the path straight on towards Brockwell. Follow the Brockwell track and in the woods take the left hand fork to follow an old stone wall. Keep going down this track passing by a signpost and following the bridleway to Brockwell. Gradually the path thins and enters a birch wood. As you enter a small clearing there is a red earth track off to the left down a slope. Follow this down and you will come out by the National Trust sign from which you started.

Horner Hill
2¼ miles (3.5 kms)

Start: Webber's Post car park, OS map ref: SS903438

This is the second of the walks on the National Trust Holnicote Estate and is a lot less strenuous than Walk 17. It is just long enough to put an edge on the appetite for a picnic at Webber's Post, which must be one of the most beautiful areas set aside for car parking in the whole of Exmoor National Park.

To find the start point from the A39, turn off ¾ mile east of Porlock onto the road signposted to Horner. Go through Horner Green and at the next crossroads (Chapel Cross) turn right towards Cloutsham and 200 yards further on pull onto the car park on the right.

Alternatively, travelling from Wheddon Cross on the Exford road, fork right to Dunkery about ½ mile from Wheddon Cross. Go over the cattle grid at Dunkery Gate, travel over the, top of the hill and slowly descend to the junction. There is a very sharp left turn onto the Cloutsham road, with the car park just afterwards on the right.

Walk to the viewpoint and interpretation board on the edge of the parking area, and look down into the Horner valley. The dense oak coppice woods are preserved as a unique Site of Special Scientific Interest and National Nature Reserve.

Our path leaves the car park at another information board which marks the start of an easy access trail. Follow this trail, taking the left fork to pass a stone bench. Keep straight on until the easy access trail bends right at a wooden bench. Here, leave the trail following the sign to Horner. A broad track takes you on through a pine plantation to emerge at the Jubilee Hut.

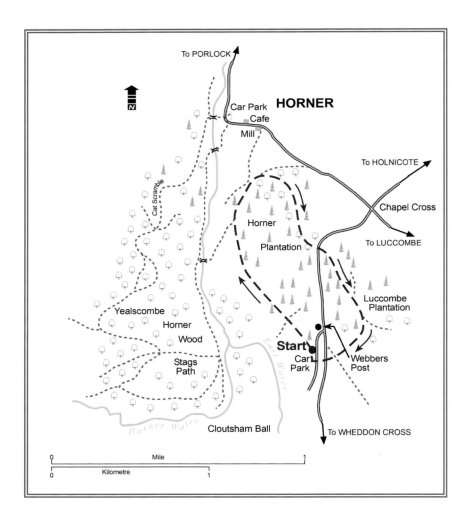

This is a magnificent viewpoint over the Horner and East Water Valleys with Dunkery Beacon and Ley Hill beyond them. Still continuing straight on the broad track, descend through pine woods, ignoring a track that branches off to the right.

Eventually a signpost is reached that points left for "Windsor

70

walk" and right for "Horner". Stop to admire the view of Crawter Hill to the left and Bossington Hill to the right, with Porlock Vale between them and the Bristol Channel beyond. Turn right here and 50 yards on turn right again signposted 'His Honour's Path to Luccombe Plantation'.

Branch left at a fork, then keep to the main path going straight on at other junctions. Continue until a vehicle barrier can be seen to your left. Cross the road at this point to continue on the broad track opposite, passing another vehicle barrier. This initially climbs, but then descends slightly to a junction. Turn right and keep to the track as it climbs to eventually meet another vehicle barrier. Keep on ahead, turning right as another track joins. Almost immediately, turn right again to pass into a parking area. Cross the road to return to Webber's Post and your car.

Horner Wood
4 miles (6.5 kms)

Start: Horner car park, OS map ref: SS898455

The next walk on the Holnicote Estate starts from the pay and display car park (free to National Trust Members) in the hamlet of Horner.

To find Horner from the Wheddon Cross direction, follow the directions given for Webber's Post in the previous walk and carry straight on when the Cloutsham road joins from the left. Go downhill across the cattle grid and turn left at the crossroads. The car park entrance is at the other end of Horner. From the A39, turn off on the road signposted to Horner ¾ mile east of Porlock and the car park is on the left just after passing the caravan park at Burrowhayes.

To start the walk, leave the car park by the vehicle entrance, turn left to walk along the road for 40 yards, and then turn right to cross the packhorse bridge over Horner Water. This is a very well preserved specimen of this type of bridge, which is built well clear of the water in order that debris brought down when the river is in full spate does not build up against the arch.

Turn right after the bridge and then after only 25 yards turn sharp left to climb up a path signposted as "Cats Scramble". Straightaway the path enters mature woodland with some very large oak and ash trees. The gradient is not too demanding, and you will soon pass through a small gate.

Still climbing, the path veers away from the stream and then swings left around the head of a more open combe with a good view of the pine trees near Webber's Post on the other side of the

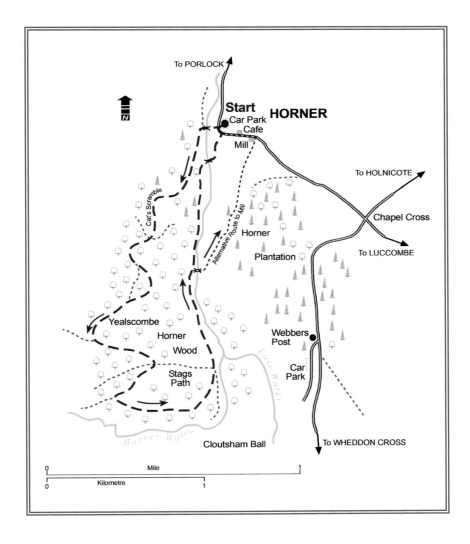

To PORLOCK

Start **HORNER**
Car Park
Cafe
Mill

To HOLNICOTE

Cat's Scramble

Alternative Route to Mill

Horner
Plantation

Chapel Cross

To LUCCOMBE

Yealscombe

Horner
Wood

Stags
Path

Webbers
Post

Car
Park

East Water

Horner Water

Cloutsham Ball

To WHEDDON CROSS

Mile
0   1

Kilometre
0   1

N

valley. Continue climbing, crossing another path. Keep straight on and the next landmark is a very welcome bench on the right.

Again the path sweeps left around the head of a wooded combe and after this the trees are nearly all coppiced oak. Keep on the main path and do not fork off on other tracks to the right. At the next signpost keep straight on, joining a path signposted as 'Granny's Ride'. There is another bench on the right, strategically placed to take advantage of magnificent views of Webber's Post to the left and Joaney How in front.

As another path joins from the right, veer left onto it to sweep round the head of wooded Yealscombe. Following the edge of this combe, the next views to the left are of Bossington Hill, Allerford and just a glimpse of Selworthy with the Beacon behind.

Soon another signpost is reached, and you continue straight on along Granny's Ride. The path contours through some magnificent oak woodland, before descending to join a wide vehicle track.

Here we leave Granny's Ride; turn sharp left on to the track known as Lord Ebrington's Path, and follow it downhill. The track provides easy downhill walking, passing through a wide vehicle turning area where it is joined by the path following Horner Water on the right.

Carry straight on to follow the stream all the way back to Horner, passing through a gate and over a stone bridge. There are two tea rooms in which to have some well earned refreshment; the car park is easily found again by turning left along the road.

East Water and Stoke Wood
4 miles (6.5 kms)

Start: Cloutsham Ford, OS map ref: SS897430

L ike the preceding walk, this one can be undertaken when the weather is unsuitable for open moorland walking and is especially useful when fog or low cloud is spoiling the visibility elsewhere. It is nearly all amongst the trees of the Holnicote Estate and offers good chances of sighting red deer and a wide variety of woodland birds. There is one quite steep climb at Prickslade Combe.

Cloutsham is reached from Webber's Post. Follow the road from there signposted to Cloutsham and park beside the road, immediately after crossing the ford.

Opposite the small car parking area there is a clearing. Pass through this, to join a stone path. Follow this, as it sticks closely to East Water - crossing six footbridges on the way! These have all been rebuilt by the National Trust to enable not only riders but walkers to keep their feet dry. Keep following the river downstream ignoring the bridleway signs and after the fifth bridge you should reach a three way signpost.

Follow the signs for Horner Combe. After crossing the sixth bridge, keep to the path nearest the stream and then cross another bridge. The next bridge is over Horner Water. To the right from this bridge can just be seen the junction of Horner and East Waters. Turn left immediately after this bridge and follow the wide track up the side of Horner Water for just 100 yards. Then take the first fork on the left and continue to follow the stream on the same side but on a

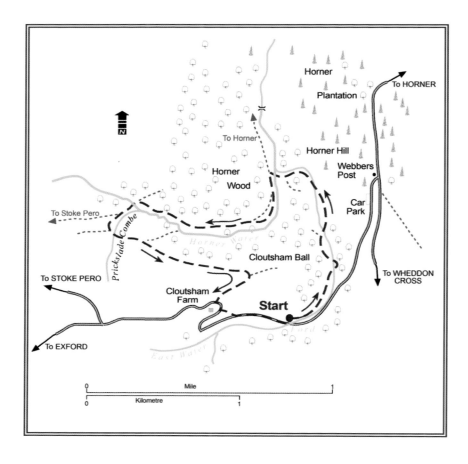

narrower path. Soon, the path rejoins a wide track again. Look out for the next footbridge on the left and cross over it.

Turn right towards Stoke Pero as indicated on the signpost and now the path climbs quite steeply away from the water. About 400 yards after the bridge take the first path sharply off to the left. This is less distinct than the Stoke Pero path but it is fairly wide and is not difficult to spot as it climbs up through the oaks beside steep-sided Prickslade Combe to the left. Before reaching the head of this combe, turn left to cross the small stream, and the path carries on through woodland with a stone wall to the right.

The highest point of this walk has now been reached and there are glimpses through the trees on the left of the beautiful Horner valley. The steep valley side immediately to the left confirms that the climb up the side of Prickslade Combe was quite an achievement!

The path descends to skirt the top of the next combe and then climbs sharply again by the side of the wall to the right. As the path emerges into the open for the first time, look immediately for a right hand fork to take you up close to the wall. Over to the left beyond Horner Woods is Porlock Vale with Bossington Hill and the sea beyond. Turn right through the next gate on the right and follow the wall on the left.

Away to the left is Dunkery Beacon with the cairns at Robin How and Joaney How further to the left again. After just one field, go through a gate and turn left into a short lane that leads to the road skirting Cloutsham Farm. The unusual appearance of this farmhouse was created a hundred years ago when an extension was built onto the existing farmhouse in the 'Swiss' style. Bear left past the farm building and onto the road heading downhill which soon comes to a sharp bend. At the apex of the hairpin bend, turn off left down a rough track and follow this down to the road and picnic area beside the water. On reaching the road carry straight on for the ford where the car is.

To Dunkery Beacon from the West
4 miles (6.5 kms)

Start: Stoke Pero Common, OS map ref: SS878427

This walk is contained within the National Trust Estate of Holnicote. It traverses open country to ascend Dunkery Beacon from the west. Again, it is recommended that this walk be undertaken on a day of good visibility, as the long distance views are a feature not to be missed. This is probably the walk where sighting a wide variety of moorland bird life is most likely. Meadow pipits and stonechats are frequently seen, ring ouzels and curlews are occasionally spotted and even the rare merlin is to be seen by a lucky few. Red deer are plentiful in the wooded combes and on the heather-covered slopes. It is rare for the observant walker not to be rewarded by a sight of these noble animals during a walk in this area.

From June onwards there is the added bonus of the fragrant heather flowering season, which climaxes in late August with masses of ling or common heather forming a carpet of pinkish purple. Before this there is the cross-leaved variety with its globular pink drooping flowers and then the bell variety, which favours drier ground and has crimson- purple, egg-shaped flowers.

The starting point is not a formal car park, but it is not difficult to find. From Exford, take the Porlock road and fork right for Stoke Pero and Cloutsham after the cattle grid. Continue towards Cloutsham for approximately 2 miles, bearing right at Porlock Post until, just before a row of fir trees on the left, there is a pole barrier across a path on the right with a signpost that indicates that this is

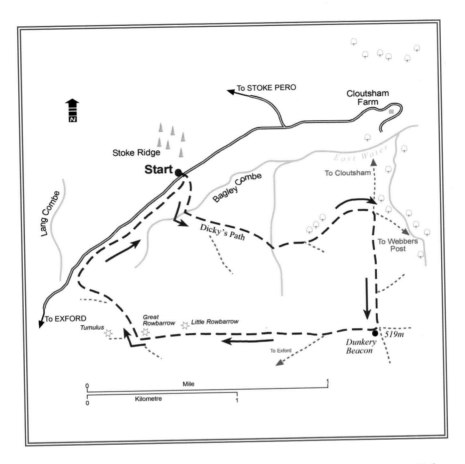

the start of Dicky's Path to Webber's Post. Park the car just off the road on the grass verge.

Follow Dicky's Path down into Bagley Combe and up the other side. From here the cairn at the summit of Dunkery Beacon cannot be seen and the two cairns immediately in front are those on top of Robin How and Joaney How. Over to the left is Selworthy Beacon and half left the islands of Flat Holm and Steep Holm can be seen in Bridgwater Bay. Ignore the path forking right to Dunkery Beacon and carry straight on. The path descends into and climbs out of another combe and then passes a row of beech trees on the left. Keep to the main track and pass to the right of two enclosures marked by posts` that are protecting Iron Age enclosures. After an easy stretch of level walking, the beeches end and it is possible to see Cloutsham Farm down below to the left and the rocks of Hurlstone Point behind. Half left are the pines of Webber's Post with Selworthy church behind.

Just before descending the next combe another path crosses Dicky's Path. Turn right onto this path and commence the real climb to Dunkery Beacon. This is a fairly steep grassy path and perhaps the most pleasant way of tackling it is in short bursts with frequent about turns to appreciate the marvellous vista to the north. The deep combe to the left of the ascent is Aller Combe. Because of the shape of the hill, the cairn at the top does not appear until 100 yards from the summit, just after the steepest part of the ascent. At the summit, the view point indicator is the best help for identifying the numerous points of interest.

The walk now sets off on the homeward journey and the next target is westward to the Rowbarrows. The cairns marking these two barrows can be seen a mile ahead. The path is quite distinct, being the right hand, or most northerly, of the two paths running from the Beacon along the ridge of the hill. Walk past Little Rowbarrow and continue until the path curves right, passing Great Rowbarrow on your right and down a grassy track leading towards a small wire enclosure. Quarter right is Porlock Hill and immediately in front is Lucott Moor draining down into Nutscale reservoir, which provides Minehead's water supply. To the left are the wide open spaces of the heart of Exmoor, north of Simonsbath.

Pass just to the left of the small enclosure that surrounds a rainfall measuring gauge and follow the path downwards to the Exford-

Cloutsham road, which it meets by a National Trust collection box at the head of Lang Combe. Turn right here to follow the road back to the start and very soon the car should be in sight again.

Over to the left is Stoke Pero with its tiny church. The church is of ancient foundation and many restorations have taken place. One of these at the end of the 19th century is commemorated by a plaque recording the service of Zulu, a Porlock donkey who carried all the roof timbers up from Porlock.

Hawkcombe
3½ miles (5.5 kms)

Start: Pittcombe Head OS map ref: SS842463

One of the best-known features for motorists visiting or passing through Exmoor is the 'fearsome' Porlock Hill. Since 1900, when this was first climbed by a motor vehicle, it has presented a challenge to hundreds of thousands of drivers. It holds no fear for the modern-day motorist but, to those who do not wish to risk being held up by a coach or juggernaut grinding up in bottom gear, there is the pleasure of using the toll road with its less severe gradients and beautiful scenery. If a caravan is being towed, the toll road gradients of 1 in 12 are more reassuring than the stretch of 1 in 4 on the main road.

This walk starts from the rough car parking area at Pittcombe Head, on the same side of the road as the AA box at the junction of the A39 and the toll road. At first follow the wide vehicle track from the car park, signposted as a bridleway to Hawkcombe Head. The track heads away from the main road towards the open moorland and runs parallel with a hedge on the right. Keep straight on, turning left just before the reaching the Porlock-Exford road, which you cross to follow the path signposted to Porlock.

This point is Hawkcombe Head and the patches of green rushes show where the springs rise to feed this combe. Here is the site of a 'knapping floor', where flints for hunting were worked by Stone Age man in the Neolithic period nearly 4000 years ago. As the path descends along the side of the combe, Porlock Vale appears in front with Bridgwater Bay beyond, and soon the top edge of Hawkcombe

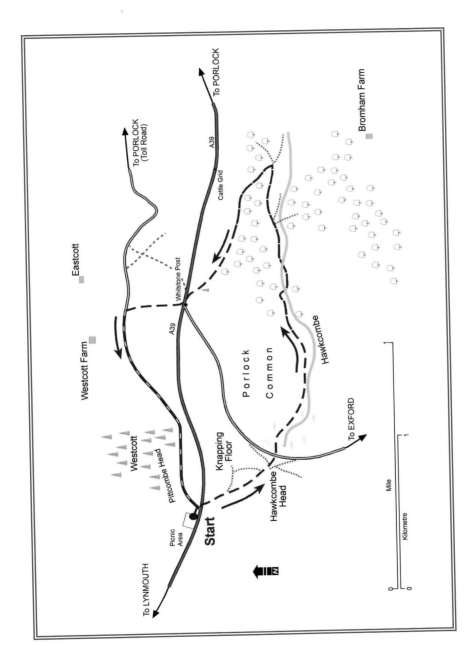

Wood is reached. Carry on descending into the woods, and when the path meets the water again, do not cross it but take the path along the bank.

Now the woodland is dense and in summertime the warblers' song is never ending. Follow the stream downwards until a track is reached just after a gate. Do not follow the blue waymarked path to Porlock but instead turn left onto a broad track. This soon fords a small stream and then continues straight on, climbing more steeply with Bromham Farm visible through the trees on the right.

As the path emerges from the trees and just before the cattle grid turn sharp left onto a narrow path through gorse, signposted to 'Whitstones'. Along this path, there are good views back along the combe that has been followed, and behind to Dunkery Beacon with the Rowbarrows to the right. The path follows the edge of the woodland as it climbs steadily upward and out onto the open common. Keep straight on through heather and gorse, heading for the Porlock road (A39) and the white signpost at its junction with the Exford road, which can be seen near the horizon in front.

Nearing the road, turn up right towards the signpost and road junction. Close to the road is a small wooden footpath sign pointing the way across the A39 and towards the toll road. Go straight across the A39, taking care as this can be a busy road, and carry straight on through the parking area. Follow the wide track heading towards the sea, which leaves from the far left corner of the car park. After a steady descent through a mass of heather with a magnificent view of Porlock Beach, Hurlstone Point and Selworthy Beacon to the right, the path strikes the toll road from Porlock to Pittcombe Head. Turn left and follow the road back to the car.

Oare Church via Badgworthy Water
3 miles (5 kms)

Start: Malmsmead car park, OS map ref: SS793478

The next walk starts from the centre of Malmsmead, which means that there will be more people in evidence than on most of the recommended walks. Malmsmead is a popular venue for all those who wish to sample the atmosphere created in the novel *Lorna Doone* and later on television. The main building in the village is the greatly extended Lorna Doone Farm on the banks of Badgworthy Water. Originally Malmsmead Farm, it was renamed after the novel but does not feature in the story. Badgworthy Water leads back to the 'water slide' at Lank Combe and Hoccombe Water with the ruined cottages of Badgworthy settlement, which have been linked with similar places in the book.

To reach Malmsmead is a minor adventure in itself with steep and narrow picturesque roads to be traversed. Turn off the A39 Porlock to Lynmouth road at either the turning to Brendon or the one near County Gate and follow the signs to Malmsmead. Alternatively, turn off the B3223 Simonsbath to Lynmouth road at Brendon Manor Farm and follow the Brendon valley road through Rockford and Brendon. Park the car in the picnic area car park (parking fee).

Leave the car park by the exit adjacent to the toilets and walk past Lorna Doone Farm. Turn left onto the Oare road and cross the bridge over Badgworthy Water. 150 yards further on turn right onto the entrance road to Cloud Farm, which is also a public footpath. This passes through fields and a small wood before running along-

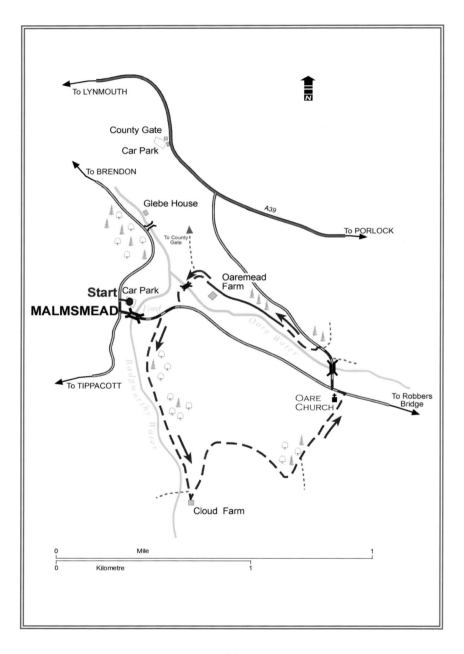

To LYNMOUTH

County Gate
Car Park

To BRENDON

Glebe House

A39

To PORLOCK

To County
Gate

Oaremead
Farm

Start Car Park
MALMSMEAD Ford

Oare Water

Badgeworthy Water

To TIPPACOTT

OARE
CHURCH

To Robbers
Bridge

Cloud Farm

| 0 | Mile | 1 |
| 0 | Kilometre | 1 |

side the water. As it crosses another cattle grid, heather topped Malmsmead Hill can be seen across to the right, and then further on Great Black Hill.

On reaching Cloud Farm, turn sharp left uphill on the path signposted to Oare Church. This passes through an open-sided shed, through a gate and then climbs back up the side of the hill above the drive which has just been walked. The wide dusty or muddy track passes through a gateway, veers off slightly right and then passes through a sheep pen. Keeping the hedge to the left, follow the yellow waymarks around the field, through another gate and around the top of a small wooded combe. Down on the left can be seen the valley of Oare Water with Oare House Allotment topped by the busy A39 on the other side.

Turn left at the head of the combe, to follow the bridleway to Oare along the edge of the trees. Go through the wooden gate into the next field and then follow the hedge on the left to the bottom of the field. Go round the garden of a house following the bridleway signs, through the gate about 40 yards in along the bottom hedge. Carry on down the side of the hedge to the road and the first glimpse is obtained of Oare church tower. On reaching the road turn left and take the opportunity of joining over 30,000 visitors per year who look round this very well maintained little church.

Oare is a very ancient settlement that is mentioned in the Domesday Book and the parish church has been there for over 800 years. It is evident that R. D. Blackmore built some of the characters in his novel *Lorna Doone*, on his personal knowledge of the people who used it in his time. His grandfather was the rector of Oare at the beginning of the 19th century. There is no obvious cashing in on the Lorna Doone legend and the visitor's attention is only discreetly drawn to the possible mechanics of the shooting scene described at the end of the novel.

On leaving the church take the Lynmouth road and cross the bridge over Oare Water. Nearly 100 yards after the bridge, turn left through wooden gates to follow a path signposted to Malmsmead. The path then passes through a plantation of larch with water just below to the left. Next in front is Oaremead Farm and the path passes to the right, following a line of power cables and through several gates.

After the gate 100 yards past the farm buildings turn left towards the water and then turn right along the river bank. Cross the concrete arch bridge and go straight on to pass Parsonage Farm on the left. Turn right on reaching the road, and you will soon be back at the Cloud Farm entrance. Return to the car park over the bridge and past Lorna Doone Farm.

The Foreland

2½ miles (4 kms)

Start: Barna Barrow car park, Countisbury, OS map ref: SS753496

Although this appears to be a short walk, it is not recommended for anyone who suffers from vertigo or is a bit short of wind, as there are high cliffs and a climb of about 800 feet in ¾ mile up from the lighthouse. However, for anyone else it is well worth while for the views from the top of Countisbury Common, 1000 feet above Lynmouth Bay.

The start point is in the National Trust car park on the north side of the A39 road from Lynmouth to Porlock. Having driven through Countisbury, turn left into the car park just after crossing the cattle grid. Before starting the walk, there is a good opportunity of looking at the surrounding area from the car park. Westwards is the town of Lynton with Hollerday Hill behind it to the right. This town was established as a holiday resort about the time of the Napoleonic Wars when it was necessary to create alternatives for those who were accustomed to travel abroad for their holidays. Its fame as the centre for North Devon beauty is now world-wide and, together with Lynmouth, it attracts visitors all the year round. Over to the left can be seen the two wooded valleys of Farley Water and Hoar Oak Water joining together, and then drawing closer to join the larger valley of the East Lyn at Watersmeet. Beyond these can be seen the high ground of the Chains, from where all these rivers except the East Lyn draw their copious supplies of water.

Start the walk by leaving the car park on the track away from the entrance and towards the sea. Keep to the wall as it swings away to

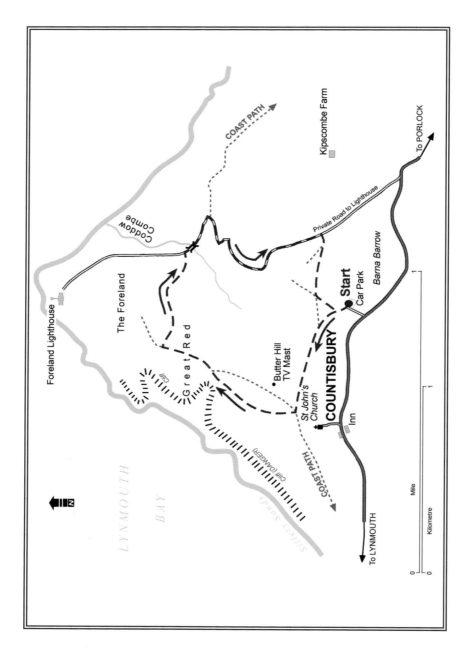

the left, joining a grassy track. Where the track turns right towards the transmitter mast, carry straight on, still following the wall. Soon, over the wall to the left can be seen the small village of Countisbury with its weather-beaten church. Then, in front is the first view of Lynmouth harbour with the cliff railway descending nearly vertically from Lynton. Originally this harbour was the base for fishing boats that caught large quantities of herring in the Bristol Channel, but these became rare 200 years ago. Later, lime and coal were landed here and one of the lime kilns is still preserved on the Esplanade.

As the path opens out on the cliff top, it joins the Coast Path. There is a four-way signpost here; turn sharp right to follow the Coast Path round Butter Hill, above Sillery Sands 800 feet below. At the top of Great Red, a precipitous gully, bear left following the Coast Path towards Porlock. At the next signpost turn right, continuing to follow the Coast Path. Again, there is a steep drop to the left of the path as it descends to join a tarmac road.

Turn right on the road, cross the bridge and start the long uphill pull. Keep to the tarmac, leaving the coast path at the first right hand bend to continue the climb. Take time to turn and enjoy the views as you pass through the hairpin bends.

As the road finally levels out, turn sharp right onto a track that has a signpost to Countisbury. Take the next left fork after about 30 yards and in front the mast on top of Countisbury Common confirms the route. Turn left at the next fork that crosses the track and this soon joins another track coming from the right that ends at car park where the walk started.

Doone Country
7½ miles (12 kms)

Start: Dry Bridge car park, Brendon Common,
OS map ref: SS759453

Awalking programme in Exmoor would not be complete without a visit to the legendary 'Doone Country'. The quick way to see the two main contenders for the 'Doone Valley' is to walk up Badgworthy Water and return the same way, but the longer route described here is a much more satisfactory achievement and it is not hard going. However, it would be best to pick a dry day with good visibility and, if there is a nip in the air, wear an extra jersey for the Brendon Common crossings.

The starting point is on the B3223 road between Simonsbath and Lynton. From Lynton, leave the A39 at Hillsford Bridge and follow the road onto Brendon Common. One mile after crossing the cattle grid onto the open common, pull into the large car park on the left. Just in case the mile-ometer is not working, this quarried out car park is the second one on the left. From Simonsbath the car park is the first quarried out one on the right about 1½ miles after crossing the cattle grid at Brendon Two Gates.

Walk 50 yards alongside the road towards Simonsbath to a sign-post indicating the path to Brendon and Malmsmead. Turn left to follow this bridleway across the open common. On the right hand side of the path is an iron 'Star of Bethlehem' sign that marks the site of a tumulus. During World War II this method of identification was used on open moorland to prevent the destruction of sites of historic interest by tracked vehicles training in the area. Keep

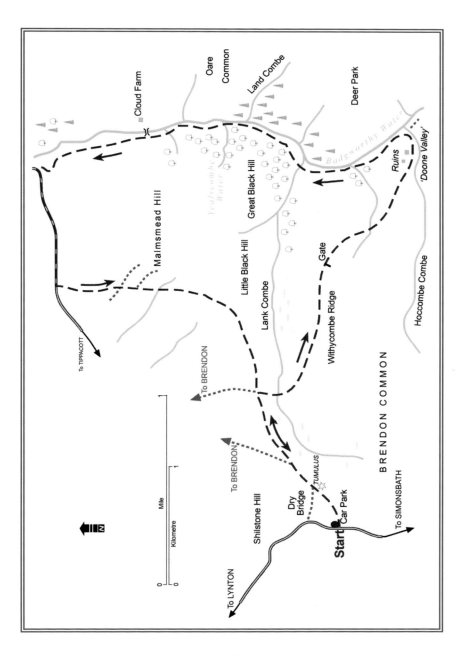

straight on and over to the right is the start of Lank Combe, which is crossed twice during this walk.

At the crossing of tracks with a four-way fingerpost, turn right towards the Doone Valley and descend into the combe. Cross the water and climb up the stony track half left on the other side to Withycombe Ridge. The path then takes a line parallel with the combe through bracken. After the bracken, look out for a path which forks slightly right to avoid a boggy stretch. This leads to a gate in the boundary wall of the common and there is a bridleway sign. If the fork is missed, do not worry unduly but fork off later on and, as long as the combe is left behind, the gate in the wall will be found. Go through this, taking special care to ensure that the gate is secure, because great inconvenience can be caused by the encroachment of commoners' stock onto the privately owned land and vice versa.

To the right now are the combes of Hoccombe and Hoccombe Water on their way down to Badgworthy Water in front. Carry straight on steadily downhill crossing the small stream running down from Withycombe Ridge. It can be seen that the bracken in this area is regularly cut for bedding. This is necessary because little straw is produced in the Exmoor region and most must be expensively imported from as far away as East Anglia.

Now the path passes through a break in the boundary wall in a row of trees into Hoccombe Combe, a contender for the title of 'Doone Valley'. There is plentiful evidence here of an old settlement, in the form of overgrown field boundaries and ruins of cottages. It is easy to appreciate the attraction of this valley as a place to live, because it is sheltered from all directions and has water, and fuel in the form of wood and peat is readily available. Walk on down past the ruins and bear to the left towards Malmsmead before reaching the water.

Now the path follows Badgworthy Water and becomes more popular the nearer it gets to Malmsmead. In front is Great Black Hill, behind the oaks of Lank Combe, and over on the other side of the water is the Deer Park. The path threads its way through the rocks of Withycombe Ridge Water (keep over to the right for the easiest way through). Then it enters dense trees and rhododendrons before the bridge over Lank Combe, another valley linked with the novel, *Lorna Doone*.

If a closer view of the 'Water Slide' is required, turn left for about 20 yards after the bridge. After heavy rain this is quite an impressive sight but television series and films of *Lorna Doone* have tended to use more dramatic locations. The path carries on through more woodland opposite Deer Park Plantation and Land Combe on the other side of the water. Go through the gate at Yealscombe Water, and again take care to see it is closed afterwards. The large barrier across the water at this point is to allow water to pass freely but stop animals getting upstream.

Continue through still more woodland and then an open level stretch below Malmsmead Hill. This is the site of the Richard Doddridge Blackmore memorial stone which was placed here in 1969 – the centenary of the publication of his novel *Lorna Doone*. The next landmark is the bridge across to Cloud Farm. Just upstream from this bridge can be seen the site of the previous bridge, which was destroyed in 1952. Do not cross the bridge but follow the bridleway towards Malmsmead, which bears left, away from the river, to go through a gate into a sunken path with a hedge on the right. Follow this path until it crosses a stream and climbs to join a metalled road. A detour can be made at this point to continue ahead down the road for the facilities and seasonal refreshments at Malmsmead. To continue the walk, turn sharp left to follow the road uphill. It climbs steadily upwards with a good view across to

Malmsmead Hill on the left.

Cross the cattle grid and before reaching the power lines, bear left at a sign post to Dry Bridge. Follow the direction indicated by the signpost down to the head of a small gully and streambed. Bear right onto the track and then, after a few yards, left onto another wide track. This descends into a shallow combe with a ford. Cross the river then take the path straight ahead up a stony track, bearing right after about 70 yards. Follow this path to a junction of many tracks then carry straight on to meet a wide vehicle track. Follow this track back to Dry Bridge, passing the turn off to the left taken at the beginning of the walk.

Hoaroak Valley and Exe Head
4½ miles (7 kms)

Start: Brendon Two Gates, OS map ref: SS765433

This walk provides a fairly easy route over one of the loneliest parts of Exmoor. During the course of this walk there are four stream crossings and boggy ground near Blackpitts. Ordinary walking boots would be quite satisfactory except during prolonged wet weather when the area is best avoided.

The start point is on the B3223 road from Simonsbath to Lynton at the cattle grid 2 ½ miles north of Simonsbath. Park on the wide firm verges either side of the road near the grid. This place, Brendon Two Gates, gets its name from the original arrangement of gates. Two gates were so arranged that whichever way the wind blew, at least one barred animals from leaving or entering the Royal Forest. The word forest did not refer to an area of trees or woodland but a term relating to the special laws that protected Crown property; in fact there were very few trees in the middle of Exmoor until the 19th century.

Looking north from the cattle grid onto the open common, one of the first objects to catch the eye is the stone monument on the high point half right. This is a memorial to Colonel R. H. Maclaren, OBE, MC who reputedly gave his life to save others when an experimental weapon misfired on this spot in 1941. Eyewitness accounts suggest that, for the sake of morale, he was made into a hero to cover up a fatal blunder.

To start the walk, go over the cattle grid onto the common and turn left (westward) to follow the stone wall which marks the north-

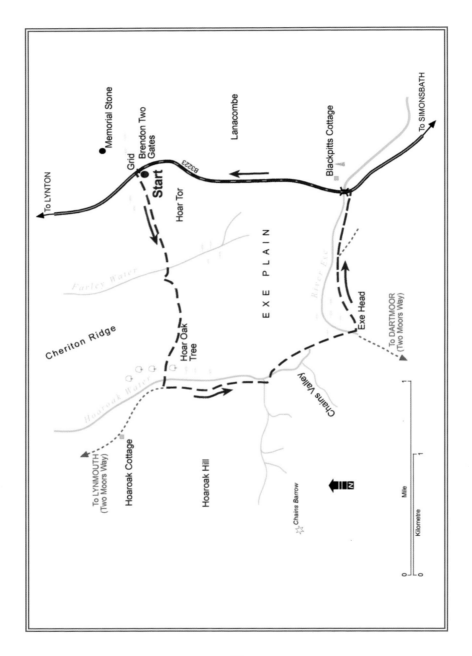

ern boundary of the old Royal Forest of Exmoor, and the boundary between Devon and Somerset. During this part of the walk it is interesting to compare the vegetation on the two sides of the wall. On the common it is typical moorland with heathers, bracken and rushes, but inside the wall Molinia grass predominates. This change was brought about by extensive drainage and burning within the former Royal Forest boundaries.

The path descends into the steep-sided combe of Farley Water and the best way up the other side is to go up to the right and then bear left again to continue following the bank. As the descent into the next combe is started, over to the right can be seen Hoaroak Cottage. Until the 1950s this was a shepherd's home but it has since been relegated to a shelter for animals. Continue to follow the wall down, but just before reaching Hoaroak Water at the bottom, turn left through a hunting gate in the wall.

Immediately in front, surrounded by railings, is the Hoar Oak tree. This is an ancient boundary mark of the Royal Forest and is the latest in a series of oak trees grown here. Although it was planted in 1917, its progress in this high, exposed situation has been very slow. Carry on down to the water, cross it, and climb up the track inside the fence to the right. On reaching the two gates at the top, do not go through either of them but turn sharp left to follow the path along the side of the valley.

This section of path is narrow but well used by walkers, as it is part of the Two Moors Way linking Dartmoor and Exmoor. A sign-post pointing the way to Exe Head lets you know that you're going the right way. The path climbs very gradually and, after passing under the ruins of a long-abandoned sheepfold and hut, the wild and rugged Long Chains Combe can be seen up to the right.

Cross the stream running out of this combe, then cross Hoaroak Water. Now the gradient becomes steeper as the path climbs up to the source of this stream, passing the gash of the Chains valley on the right. On reaching the open Exe Plain, bear right on the hard track and follow this up to the gate at Exe Head. Do not try to short cut across Exe Plain to Blackpitts, which can be seen over to the left, as the ground is very wet.

This is literally the head of the Exe river, and water collecting here makes its way via Blackpitts, Exford and Winsford to the English Channel at Exmouth. In medieval times Exe Head was an important road junction, where pack horse trains met on the old trails that ran to all points of the compass from here. Turn left at the signpost and follow the wire fence on the left.

Stay close to the fence until it turns sharply downwards to cross the infant Exe. Ignore the stile in the fence here and turn right to follow the path along and up the side of the valley. Cross the stile, following signs for Blackpitts, and after 150 yards descend to Exe Head Bridge. Go through the gate, and onto the Brendon Two Gates road. Turn left to follow this road all the way back to the car.

This is the least interesting part of the walk, but the verges are wide and it is only 20 minutes back to the car. The reason for the unusual width of this moorland road is that it is the final stretch of a vital road that was constructed between Coppleham Cross in the Exe Valley and Brendon Two Gates in 1926-33. From the beginning of the century Dulverton Rural District Council had planned to provide a highway that could bring relief to the villages of Winsford, Exford and Simonsbath during bad weather and this became possible in 1926 when the Government supplied the necessary funds to create work for the large number of unemployed men at the time.

Hoaroak Water and the East Lyn
4 miles (6.5 kms)

Start: Hillsford Bridge, OS map ref: SS741478

In August 1952 it was a miserable holiday month in the Exmoor area with rain falling incessantly on the peat bogs of the central high ground known as the Chains. On Friday 15th August this rainfall became even more intense and the streams flowing both north and south became raging torrents. Then, in the evening, a cloudburst deposited five inches of rain in an hour, making a total rainfall of nine inches in 24 hours. The rivers running north to Lynmouth drop very quickly to the sea, and the force of water and massive boulders tearing down the East and West Lyn rivers caused a terrible disaster, with the loss of 34 lives.

This walk follows two of the rivers and it will not be difficult to imagine the horror when their valleys were full of water and debris. Hillsford Bridge was washed away that night and was temporarily replaced by a Bailey bridge built by the Army. Later this was replaced by the construction to be seen today. The bridge crosses Hoaroak Water just as the B3223 road from Simonsbath joins the A39 above Lynmouth. To park the car, drive into the Combe Park entrance gate and use the National Trust car park immediately on the left.

Leave the car park, turning right and walking across Hillsford Bridge. Turn in through the first gate on the left to walk down the side of Hoaroak Water following bridleway signs for Watersmeet. The wide track follows the rapid descent of Hoaroak Water through oak woodland. The series of waterfalls amongst the vast boulders

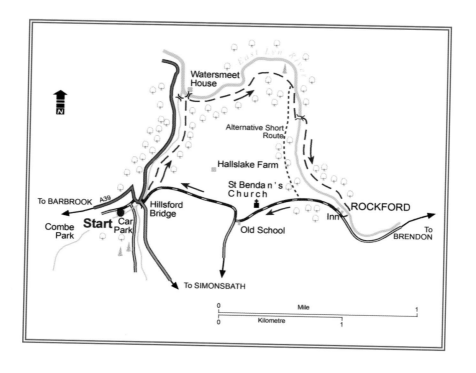

are an impressive sight, especially in winter months or after a summer storm up in the moors. As the valley temporarily widens there is a glimpse of open South Hill Common above the steep cleave in front. Then it narrows again and there is a short track down to the left where one of the waterfalls can be viewed at close quarters.

Further on, the track bends to the right, and a zigzag path from Watersmeet car park comes down on the other side of the river to cross a bridge below to the left. Fork left down steep steps to the near end of this bridge. Do not cross it, but certainly take time to watch the antics of the dippers that are usually active on the boulders below. Turn right towards Watersmeet House and, keeping to this side of the East Lyn river, walk towards Rockford. At the house there is a National Trust shop and a café, which must be one of the most beautifully situated of their properties.

The East Lyn does not descend as quickly as Hoaroak Water and migratory salmon are able to swim up this river from the sea to spawn in the upper reaches of Oare Water and Badgworthy Water. The ruins of a lime kiln are passed on the left. A little further on, as the path rises to an impressive height above the water, it is possible to look forwards up the valley to see traffic travelling along the A39 high above. Then there is a seat on the right with a magnificent view through the trees towards Barton Wood. Just after this seat there is a choice of paths to Rockford. Keep straight on at this point following the footpath sign for Rockford.

Now the path descends through an area of dense woodland. As it comes to the river again, there is the tranquil Horner's Pool down to the left, where the river has taken a devious route around a rocky outcrop. This is one of the many named pools where the fishermen try to outwit the wily salmon and trout. A little further on, cross the bridge and then turn right to follow the river upstream again. Near the top of this climb there is a well positioned seat. At the next seat, the path is nearly at water level and the river is running through a rocky channel between peaceful pools where large numbers of trout can normally be seen in the clear water.

Now the first buildings of Rockford appear on the opposite bank. The origin of the place name is obvious from the condition of the river here as it widens out to find a way round large polished rocks. Do not cross the ford but take the path between the river and Rockford Lodge to the bridge. Cross the bridge and then turn right to walk along the road through the hamlet with its inn. There is a steep climb up the road, passing cottages on the right set in beautiful positions above the river. Keep straight on up the road on a steeper hill with the church tower of St Brendan's in front as a target. It was built here in 1738 to replace another church which was the other side of Farley Water, three miles from the village. Some of the stone was removed from the old church together with the sundial that can be seen over the porch.

As the road turns to the right the worst of the climb is over. Pass the old school on the left, and at the next T-junction, turn right to follow a road signposted to Hallslake. This leads all the way back to the start point at Hillsford Bridge.

The Valley of Rocks and Lee Valley
5 miles or 2½ miles (8 kms or 4 kms)

**Start: Valley of Rocks, Lynton, OS map ref: SS710497,
or Lee Bay, OS map ref: SS695492**

The Valley of Rocks, west of Lynton is one of those places that must be seen to be believed. Somehow, photographs never seem to capture the unusual atmosphere created by the weird rock formations and steep cleaves. It is believed that this was not always a dry valley and thousands of years ago, when the sea level was much higher, this could well have been part of the original exit to the sea of the Lyn rivers. The precarious looking rock formations have been chiselled out by countless years of weathering action on the mixture of sandstones, slates and limestone that make up the rock strata, in particular through frost weathering in the Ice Age.

If the shorter walk is selected, drive through the Valley of Rocks, past Lee Abbey and down to the car park above the toilets at Lee Bay but, if the longer distance is chosen, park in the National Park Authority's picnic area on the left hand side of the road just before the cricket ground in the valley. In either case the walks can be conveniently shortened by a mile at a later stage. The directions start from the car park for the longer distance.

Turn left out of the car park to pass the public conveniences on the left. Take the footpath on the right hand side of the road, which passes the cricket field, a café and the public car park. Up above to the right is the rock formation known as Rugged Jack. Then there is a gap in the rocks where the cliff path from Lynton enters the valley

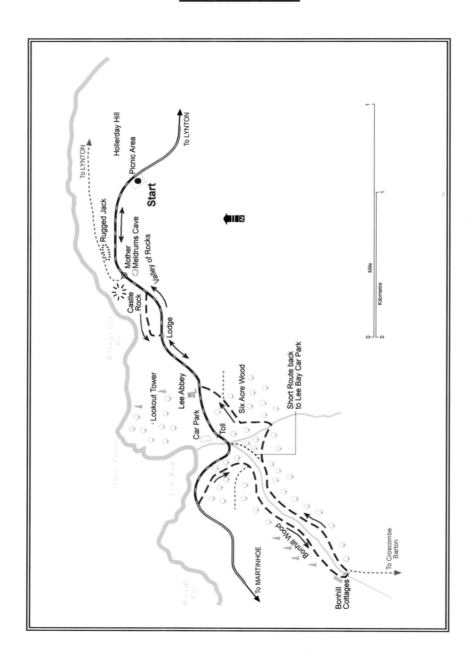

before Castle Rock, the very prominent outcrop in front. Look out for the wild goats, which are usually to be seen in this area.

Carry on along the road, straight across the roundabout, and over to the left are the rocks known as the Devil's Cheesewring, with a signpost to Mother Meldrum's cave. This lady was the legendary seer who was visited by John Ridd in R. D. Blackmore's *Lorna Doone*. You will have to imagine her cave as the fallen rocks provide little shelter. About 50 yards beyond, fork right onto a path running above Wringcliff Bay down to the right. This path ends at a wall. Turn left here to follow a path running alongside this wall back up to the road again, joining it at the Lodge.

Follow the road again, using the wide grass verge on the left hand side to make for safer walking. On the right is Lee Abbey Youth Centre and then Lee Abbey itself. Now there is a descent to the toll gate with Lee Bay down to the right. This is the starting point for those taking the shorter walk. Keep to the road passing Lee Cottage on the right and climbing up above the bay. Looking across to the right, there is the lookout tower in Cuddycleave Wood above Duty Point. As the road emerges into the open there is a perfect view of Woody Bay in front.

At this point turn sharp left off the road, to follow a wide track signposted as a bridleway to Croscombe Barton. This passes through Bonhill Wood, the gradient decreases and there is evidence of active woodland management. Along here it is possible to shorten the walk by a mile if the signposted route for the Woodland Walk to Lee Abbey is followed. Take the second left turn, downhill to cross a vehicular bridge, and then turn left to rejoin the main walk.

If following the planned walk, carry straight on, and soon there are narrow, lush meadows down to the left, before reaching Bonhill Cottages on the right. Turn sharp left over the bridge in front of these cottages and then, at the top of a short climb, fork left to climb over a stile to follow the footpath signposted to Lee Abbey. This is a very different kind of path and care is needed over the first 200 yards or so. Just after the stile there is a derelict building. Pass to the left of this and then turn sharp right at the end of the shed to climb up some rock steps.

The path descends to cross a footbridge over a small stream and up steps on the other side. From here the path is more prominent through wild woodland, and it runs parallel with the track previously followed on the other side of the stream. Be prepared to clamber over or round the occasional fallen tree along this path. Fork left downhill on the occasion where there is a choice of paths and, as the path descends nearly to water level, it passes a wide vehicular bridge where the shortened woodland walk rejoins.

If the car is parked at Lee Bay car park, fork left a few yards after the footbridge across the Lee Stream onto a signposted footpath. This follows the Lee Stream and emerges onto the road just by Lee Cottage. Otherwise carry straight on and very soon Lee Abbey can be seen through the trees. The track swings right and then turns left over a bridge near the head of a combe. When the path forks, take the left and in a few yards Lee Bay can be seen down below. As the path leaves the woods it rejoins the toll road opposite the entrance to Lee Abbey. Turn right to retrace the early part of the walk back to the picnic area car park.

Heddon's Mouth
2 miles (3 kms)

Start: Hunter's Inn, OS map ref: SS653480

On Exmoor it is very difficult to plan a circular walk without an appreciable gradient at some stage, and, on looking back through the previous walks, it must be admitted that they all contain at least one significant ascent. This last walk though is short and nearly level, in spectacular surroundings.

The easiest way of reaching the starting point by car is to travel on the A399 from Blackmoor Gate towards Combe Martin for two miles and then turn off right on the turning signposted to Trentishoe and Hunter's Inn. There is an added bonus here in the form of a spectacular journey over the last two miles of this route. It is also possible to leave the A39 just north of the turning to Parracombe but this is a very narrow and steep road which can involve much reversing! At Hunter's Inn there is the hotel itself, National Trust shop and Visitor Centre and public toilets. The car park is opposite the toilets.

To start the walk, go down the road towards the inn. For many years this has been home to peacocks, the males of which occasionally see their reflections in cars and attack them as intruders. Fork right just before the front of the inn and then take the wide footpath immediately alongside it. Go through the gate and then fork left for the path to Heddon's Mouth Beach. The path follows the River Heddon, originally only known by this name after the meeting of the Parracombe and Trentishoe Waters below the inn.

As the path starts to rise in Road Wood there is a choice of paths.

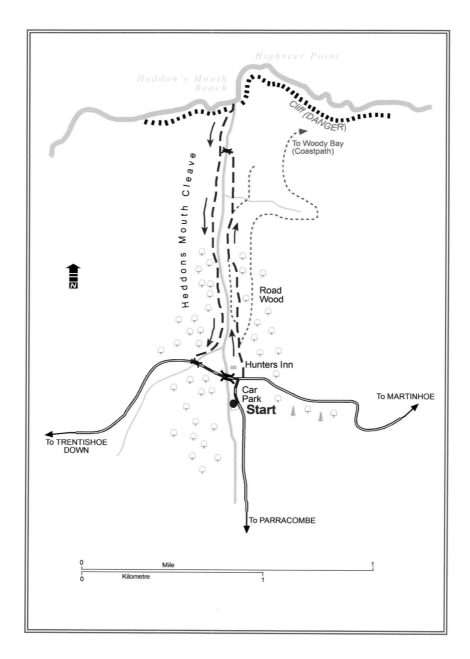

Highveer Point

Heddon's Mouth
Beach

Cliff (DANGER)

To Woody Bay
(Coastpath)

Heddons Mouth Cleave

N

Road
Wood

Hunters Inn

Car
Park
Start

To MARTINHOE

To TRENTISHOE
DOWN

To PARRACOMBE

0   Mile   1
0   Kilometre   1

Either stay on the path that goes through the oaks at a higher level or take the narrower lower path near the river bank, which can be damp in places. The paths rejoin where there is a bridge, but do not cross. Continue down the valley, and as open ground is reached, there is a startling view of Heddon's Mouth Cleave on the other side of the river. This rises steeply to a height of 700 feet. As the path gets nearer to the mouth of the river it will be noticed that the trees become more and more stunted as they become exposed to the wind from the sea. Keep straight on where the Coast Path to Woody Bay forks off to the right.

Hill Brook is crossed and up above to the right can be seen a path making its way along the side of the steep valley down which this brook descends. This path follows the route of an old carriage road that ran from Hunter's Inn to Woody Bay, past the site of a Roman signalling station and nearly 700 feet above the jagged rocks between Highveer Point and Wringapeak.

As the next bridge across the river is approached, the rocky shambles of Highveer Point can be seen to the right. Cross the bridge here and turn right for the beach. With care it is possible to swim from this beach and years ago it was used for landing cargo from coasters. Limestone which was landed here was burnt in the lime kiln on the edge of the beach. Lime is essential to sweeten the predominantly acid ground on Exmoor and, before the present road system was constructed, it was always more convenient to bring in the limestone and fuel to the nearest landing point on the coast.

The path now returns on the same route to the bridge but continue ahead without crossing the bridge. After passing through an open area there is a dry stone wall on the left that separates the scree from the mixed woodlands of water-loving trees, including among others ash and alder, together with sycamore, beech, birch and elder. As it enters an ash wood the path becomes nearly enclosed for a short stretch by a hedge on the left above verdant meadows. This is replaced by a stone wall and now there is a lot of hart's tongue fern on both sides of the path.

As the hotel comes into sight, the path veers off to the right and after passing a memorial garden - 'Harry's Orchard' on the left - goes through a gate onto Trentishoe road. Turn sharp left to follow the road over two bridges back to Hunter's Inn and the car park.